FRANCE TRAVEL GUIDE 2023:
An Amazing Travel Guide on How to Enjoy Your Stay in France

Quincy Allaire

All rights reserved. No part of this publication may be reproduced, distributed, or transmitted in any form or by any means, including photocopying, recording, or other electronic or mechanical methods without prior written permission of the publisher, except in the case of brief quotations embodied in critical reviews and certain other noncommercial uses permitted by copyright law.

Copyright © Quincy Allaire, 2023.

Table of contents

A Brief History of France
Geography Of France
Requirements For Traveling To France
Places To Visit When In France
Planning Your Trip To France
Getting Around In France
Accommodations In France
Food And Drink
Sightseeing
Culture And Customs
Language
Safety and health
Weather
Are you visiting France as a couple? Here are some cool places for lovers that you might want to check out.
Basilica of St. Michael
Eiffel Tower
Palais Garnier Opera House
Louvre Museum

- Notre Dame Cathedral
- Palace Of Versaille
- Mont Saint-Michel
- Disneyland Paris
- Seine Cruise
- La Cote des Basques
- Arc De Triomphe
- Grand Théâtre de Bordeaux
- Promenade des Anglais
- Castle Hill
- Place Garibaldi
- Pont Alexandre III
- Museum of Fine Arts of Lyon
- Notre-Dame de la Garde
- Abbey of Saint-Victor de Marseille
- MuCEM
- Petit Trianon
- Cathédrale Saint-André
- Place de la Bourse
- Colline de la Croix-Rousse
- Fountains of Versailles
- Musee D'Orsay
- Sainte-Chapelle

Montmartre
Musee Rodin
Luxembourg Palace
Place De La Concorde
Musée de l'Orangerie
Pere Lachaise Cemetery
Palais Garnier Opera House
Boulevards Legendary Cafés
Place Massena
St Nicholas Orthodox Cathedral
Parc Phoenix
Musee National Marc Chagall
Nice Observatory
Old Nice (Vieille Ville)
Museum of modern and contemporary art
Cimiez Monastery
Basilique Notre Dame de Fourvière
Place Bellecour
Parc de La Tête d'Or
Miniature museum and theater
Cathedral Saint Jean Baptiste
Zoo De Lyon

**Money-saving Tips For You
What to expect when you are in
France.**

A Brief History of France

France has a rich and complex history that dates back to ancient times. If you're planning a trip to France for the first time, understanding some of the key events and periods in the country's history can help you appreciate the culture, architecture, and landmarks you'll encounter.

France's earliest recorded history dates back to the Celtic tribes that settled in the region around 600 BC. The Romans conquered Gaul (the Roman name for France) in the 1st century BC, and the Roman Empire controlled the area for several centuries. During this period, the Romans built many of the roads, aqueducts, and other infrastructure that can still be seen in France today.

In the 5th century AD, the Germanic tribes known as the Franks conquered the Roman province of Gaul, and their leader, Clovis, established the Merovingian dynasty.
This began the period of French history known as the Middle Ages, during which the French monarchy and the Catholic Church were the dominant powers.

During the High Middle Ages (1000-1300), the French monarchy became one of the most powerful in Europe, and the French language and culture began to emerge. In the 14th and 15th centuries, the French monarchy experienced a period of instability, with the Hundred Years' War between France and England and the outbreak of the Black Death.

The French Renaissance, which began in the 16th century, saw a resurgence of art, literature, and culture. This period also saw the rise of powerful French monarchs such as Francis I and Henry IV, who expanded the French territories and strengthened the French monarchy.

The 17th century was marked by the reign of Louis XIV, known as the Sun King, who established an absolute monarchy and built the Palace of Versailles. The 18th century saw the French Enlightenment, a period of intellectual and cultural growth that laid the foundation for the French Revolution of 1789.

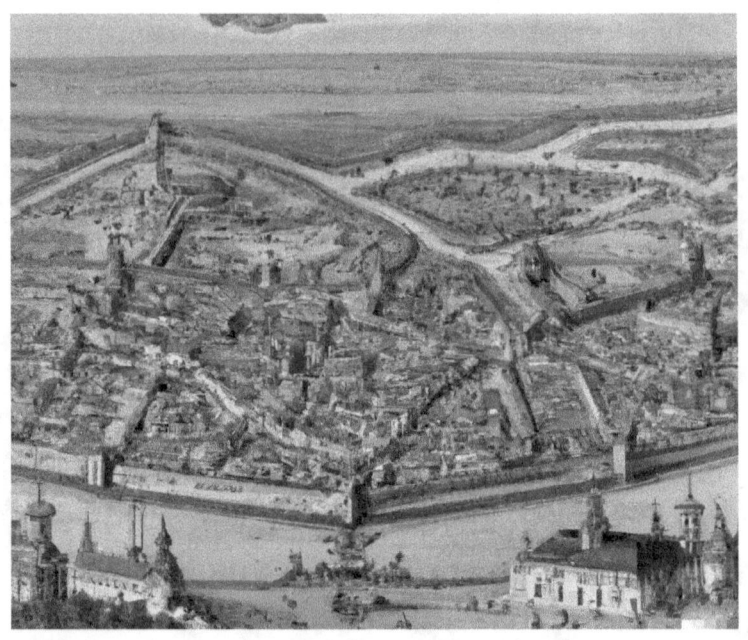
17th century view of France

The French Revolution brought about the end of the monarchy and the establishment of the First French Republic. This period also saw the rise of Napoleon Bonaparte, who established himself as Emperor of France and embarked on a series of military campaigns that expanded the French Empire.

The 19th and 20th centuries were marked by political turmoil, including the rise of the Third Republic, the two World Wars, and the Occupation of France by Germany during World War II. After the war, France experienced a period of economic growth

and social change, and the country became a republic again.

France's history is a fascinating and complex tapestry that includes periods of great achievement and innovation as well as periods of conflict and upheaval. Understanding this history can help you appreciate the culture and landmarks you'll encounter on your trip to France.

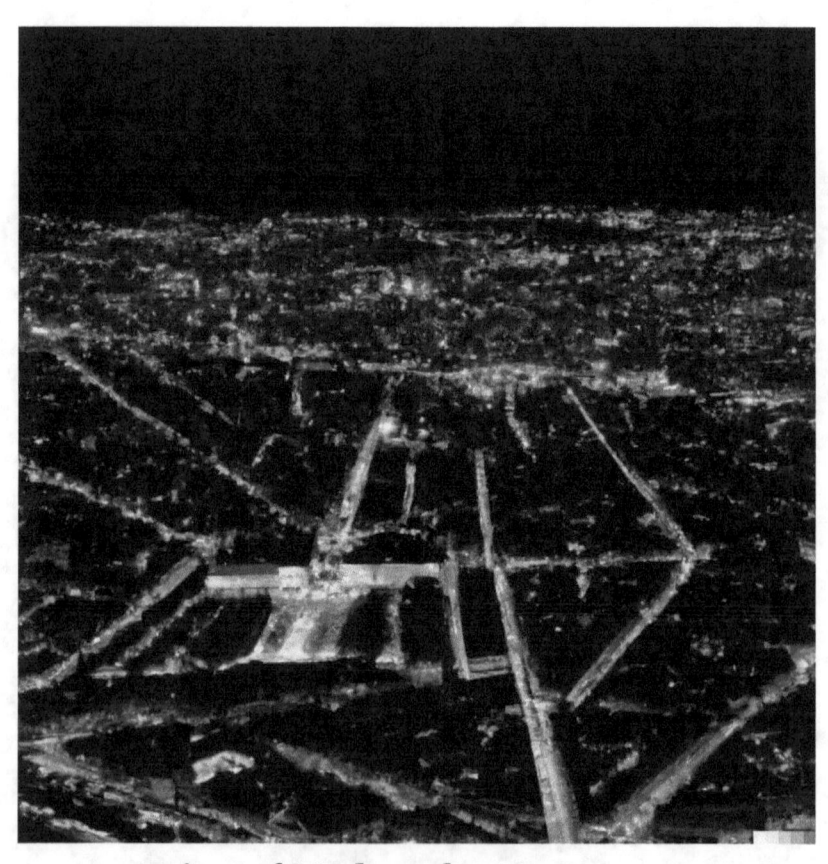

A view of Modern day France

Geography Of France

France is a country located in Western Europe and is the largest Western European country by land area. The country is bordered by Belgium, Luxembourg, Germany, Switzerland, Italy, Spain, Andorra, and the Mediterranean Sea. The total area of France is approximately 643,857 square kilometers, making it the 42nd largest country in the world.

France is divided into 13 regions, 96 departments and thousands of municipalities. The country is made up of a diverse range of geographical features including coastlines, mountains, forests, and rivers.

One of the most famous geographical features of France is the French Riviera, also known as the Côte d'Azur, which stretches along the Mediterranean coast from the Italian border to Saint-Tropez. The area is known for its picturesque beaches, glamourous resorts, and mild climate.

Another notable geographical feature of France is the Alps, which form the border between France and Italy and Switzerland. The highest peak in the French Alps is Mont Blanc, which stands at 4,810 meters tall. The Alps are popular with skiers, hikers, and climbers, and are also home to many alpine villages and resorts.

France is also home to the Massif Central, a large mountainous region located in the heart of the country. The region is known for its volcanic landscapes and is home to the Puy de Dome, the highest volcano in France.

France also has a vast network of rivers and canals, the most famous being the River Seine, which runs through the heart of Paris and is lined with famous landmarks such as Notre Dame Cathedral and the Eiffel Tower. The River Loire, which runs through central France, is also an important river and is known for its picturesque chateaux.

The geography of France is diverse and varied, from the Mediterranean beaches and glamor of the French Riviera to the rugged peaks of the Alps and the Massif Central, France has something for everyone.
The country's diverse geography has played a key role in shaping its culture, economy, and history, making it a fascinating and endlessly fascinating place to explore.

Requirements For Traveling To France

When traveling to France either a tourist or a first time traveler, there are a few essential items that you should bring with you to make your trip more comfortable and enjoyable.

1.Passport: Make sure your passport is up to date and valid for at least six months after your planned return date. This is a requirement for entry into France.

2.Travel adapter: French electrical outlets use a different type of plug than those used in the US, so you'll need a travel adapter to charge your devices.

3. Comfortable walking shoes: France is known for its beautiful cities and charming villages, and you'll likely want to do a lot of walking to explore them. Make sure to bring a pair of comfortable walking shoes to make the most of your trip.

4. Water bottle: Tap water is safe to drink in France, so bring a reusable water bottle and fill it up as needed. This can save you money and help you stay hydrated.

5. Travel insurance: While no one expects things to go wrong, it's always a good idea to have travel insurance in case of an emergency. Make sure to purchase a policy that covers you for the duration of your trip.

6. Cash and Credit Card: While many places in France accept credit cards, it's still a good idea to carry some cash with you, especially if you plan to visit smaller towns or rural areas. Also, it's a good idea to carry a credit card for emergencies.

7. Basic French phrasebook: Knowing a few basic French phrases can make a big difference in your interactions with locals, and can help you navigate your way around the country.

8. Camera: France is home to many beautiful and iconic landmarks, so don't forget to bring your camera to capture the memories of your trip.

By keeping these items in mind, you can be sure that you have everything you need for a comfortable and enjoyable trip to France.

Places To Visit When In France

France is known for its rich history, culture, and stunning landmarks, making it a popular destination for travelers. Here are some places you should consider visiting when you arrive in France:

Paris: Known as the "City of Lights," Paris is home to some of the world's most famous landmarks, including the Eiffel Tower, Notre Dame Cathedral, and the Louvre Museum.

The French Riviera: The French Riviera, or Côte d'Azur, is a popular destination for its beautiful beaches, clear waters and the famous towns like Nice, Cannes and Saint-Tropez.

The Loire Valley: This region is known for its picturesque castles, including the Château de Chambord and the Château de Chenonceau. It's also a great place to explore the French countryside and sample local wines.

Normandy: This region is famous for its World War II history and the beaches of D-Day. Visitors can also visit the famous Monastery of Mont Saint-Michel, which is located on an island off the coast of Normandy.

The Alsace Region: This region is known for its beautiful towns like Colmar, Strasbourg and Mulhouse, and also for its rich culture and history, and famous for the Alsace wines.

The French Alps: The French Alps offer a great destination for outdoor activities such as skiing, hiking, and mountaineering. The most famous towns are Chamonix, Megève and Courchevel.

Bordeaux: This city is known for its wine production and historic architecture, including the 18th-century Place de la Bourse and the Gothic Cathédrale Saint-André.

These are just a few of the many destinations you can visit in France. In this guide you would find over 90 places that might interest you to visit. You can make your choices and it also contains beautiful pictures. To make the most of your trip, you may want to prioritize what you want to see and plan your itinerary accordingly.

Planning Your Trip To France

This section would include information on visa requirements, transportation options, and suggested itineraries for different regions of France.

Planning a trip to France for a first-time traveler can be an exciting and overwhelming experience. To ensure that your trip goes smoothly, it's important to do some research and planning in advance.

First, you'll need to check the visa requirements for U.S citizens traveling to France. Generally, U.S citizens can enter France for up to 90 days without a visa for tourist or business purposes. However, it's always a good idea to check the most recent information and regulations from the French embassy or consulate before you leave.

Next, you'll want to consider your transportation options. France has an extensive train network, which is a convenient and efficient way to travel around the country. Alternatively, you can also rent a car, but keep in mind that driving in France can be challenging, especially if you're not used to driving on the right-hand side of the road.

When it comes to accommodation, France offers a wide variety of options, from budget-friendly hostels to luxurious hotels. Research your options and choose the one that best suits your needs and budget.

Food and drink is an essential part of any French experience, so make sure to indulge in the local delicacies while you're there. Be sure to try classic French dishes such as croissants, escargots, and ratatouille, and of course to taste the famous French wines.

When it comes to sightseeing, France has an abundance of attractions to choose from. The Eiffel Tower, the Louvre, and Notre-Dame are among the most famous landmarks in Paris. Also, there are many other charming towns such as Strasbourg, Nice, and Bordeaux that are worth visiting.

When it comes to culture and customs, France is a very polite society, and it's important to be aware of basic French customs and etiquette. For example, it's considered rude to speak loudly in public or to start eating before everyone at the table has been served.

Finally, safety is always a concern when traveling abroad. Make copies of your passport and important documents and keep them in a safe place. It's also a good idea to purchase travel insurance that covers you for the duration of your trip.

By keeping these things in mind, you can be sure to make the most of your trip to France and have an unforgettable experience.

Getting Around In France

Information on transportation options such as trains, buses, and cars, including tips on how to purchase tickets and navigate the various transportation systems in France.

France is a popular destination for tourists, and getting around the country is relatively easy thanks to its well-developed transportation system. Whether you're traveling by train, bus, or car, there are plenty of options to choose from.

Train Travel:
France's train system, known as the SNCF, is one of the most efficient and convenient ways to get around the country. The high-speed TGV trains connect major cities such as Paris, Lyon, Marseille, and Strasbourg, and are a great option for long-distance travel. The Regional Express Trains (TER) are another option for travel within the regions. Both options offer online booking and purchasing of tickets.

Bus Travel:
While not as popular as train travel, bus travel is still a viable option for getting around France. The main bus companies are Flixbus and Ouibus. They offer affordable and convenient travel between major cities and towns, and can be a great option for those on a budget.

Car Travel:
Renting a car can be a great way to explore the French countryside and visit small towns and villages that are not easily accessible by public transportation. However, it's important to keep in mind that driving in France can be challenging, especially if you're not used to driving on the right-hand side of the road. Also, be aware of the heavy traffic in cities like Paris and Lyon.

Bicycle Travel:
France is a great country for cycling, with many dedicated bike lanes, and bike rental services available in major cities. It's a great way to explore the smaller towns and villages and also a sustainable option.

Walking:

Many cities and towns in France are easily explored on foot. This allows you to take in the sights and sounds of the area at your own pace and discover hidden gems along the way.

No matter what mode of transportation you choose, it's important to plan ahead and purchase tickets in advance to avoid any last-minute stress. Keep in mind that during peak season, transportation can be crowded, so it's a good idea to book early.

France offers a variety of transportation options to suit the needs and preferences of different travelers. Whether you prefer the speed and convenience of train travel or the flexibility of renting a car, you're sure to find a way to get around the country that works for you.

Accommodations In France

Information on different types of accommodation options available in France, such as hotels, guesthouses, and vacation rentals, as well as tips on how to find the best deals.

France offers a wide variety of accommodation options to suit the needs and budgets of different travelers. Whether you're looking for a luxurious hotel, a cozy guesthouse, or a budget-friendly hostel, you're sure to find something that suits your needs. Here's a guide to the different types of accommodation available in France for first-time travelers:

Hotels: France is home to a wide variety of hotels, from budget-friendly options to luxury five-star establishments. Many hotels offer modern amenities such as free Wi-Fi, air conditioning, and on-site restaurants. Hotels can be found in all major cities and towns and it's a good idea to book in advance during peak season.

Guesthouses: Guesthouses are a popular option for travelers looking for a more authentic experience. Many guesthouses are run by local families and offer a more personal touch than hotels. They often have fewer rooms and provide a cozy and homely atmosphere.

Vacation rentals: Vacation rentals such as apartments and villas can offer a more independent and private option for travelers. They are a great option for families or groups of friends and offer the convenience of having a kitchen and living space.

Hostels: Hostels are a budget-friendly option for travelers. They provide dormitory-style accommodation and shared facilities such as bathrooms and kitchens. Hostels are a great option for solo travelers or backpackers and can be found in most major cities and towns.

Campsites: France is home to many campgrounds and RV parks, which can be a great option for travelers looking to experience the great outdoors. They offer a variety of accommodation options, from basic tent sites to luxury RV rentals.

When choosing your accommodation, it's important to consider your budget, location, and travel style. Research different options and read reviews to get a sense of what to expect. It's also a good idea to book in advance, especially during peak season.

France offers a wide range of accommodation options for first-time travelers. From luxurious hotels to budget-friendly hostels, you're sure to find something that suits your needs and budget. Be sure to research different options and book in advance to make the most of your trip.

Food And Drink

A guide to French cuisine, including information on regional specialties, popular dishes and recommended restaurants would also be made available in Vol. 2. Also, information on French wines, cheeses and traditional recipes. France is known for its rich culinary traditions and is a paradise for food and drink lovers. From classic French dishes to local specialties, there's something for everyone to enjoy. Here's a guide to the food and drinks you can expect to find in France as a first-time U.S traveler:

Bread: French bread is famous all over the world for its delicious taste and texture. From the classic baguette to the flaky croissant, French bread is a staple in every meal.

Cheese: France is home to hundreds of different types of cheese, from the creamy Camembert to the sharp Roquefort. Cheese is often served as a starter or as part of a cheese platter, and is often paired with wine.

Wine: France is one of the world's leading wine-producing countries, with regions such as Bordeaux, Burgundy, and Champagne producing some of the finest wines in the world. Wine is often served with meals and is a fundamental part of French culture.

Classic French dishes: France is famous for its classic dishes such as Coq au Vin, Ratatouille, and Escargots. These dishes are often rich in flavor and are made with fresh, locally sourced ingredients.

Regional specialties: Each region of France has its own unique culinary traditions and specialties. For example, in the south of France, you'll find dishes such as Bouillabaisse, a fish stew, and in the north, dishes such as the famous French onion soup.

Pastries: France is famous for its pastries, including macarons, éclairs, and tarts. These sweet treats can be found in patisseries all over the country and make for a delicious dessert or snack.

Coffee and tea: France is also known for its coffee and tea culture. A traditional French cafe experience is a must-try for any traveler, where you can enjoy a cup of coffee or tea accompanied by a croissant or pastry.

When it comes to drinking, it's important to note that the legal drinking age in France is 18 years old. If you're planning to indulge in wine or other alcoholic beverages, be sure to do so responsibly and in moderation.

There are rich and diverse culinary experiences for first-time U.S travelers to France. From the classic French dishes to the local specialties, the country's food and drink is an essential part of French culture. Don't forget to pair your meal with a glass of wine and enjoy the culinary traditions that make France a top destination for foodies.

Sightseeing

A guide to the top attractions and landmarks in France, including historical sites, museums, and natural wonders. Information on opening times, admission fees and how to avoid the crowds.

France is a beautiful country with a rich history and culture. It's no wonder that it's a popular destination for tourists from all over the world, including the United States. If you're planning a trip to France for the first time, there are a few things you should know to make the most of your sightseeing experience.

One of the top things to see in France is the Eiffel Tower. This iconic structure is located in the heart of Paris and offers breathtaking views of the city. Visitors can take a tour to the top of the tower or simply admire it from the ground. Nearby, you'll also find the Arc de Triomphe and the Champs-Élysées, two other popular Parisian landmarks.

Another must-see destination in France is the Palace of Versailles. This grand palace was the residence of the French monarchy during the 17th and 18th centuries. Visitors can tour the palace, gardens and the famous Hall of Mirrors.

The French Riviera, also known as the Côte d'Azur, is a popular destination for its beautiful beaches and picturesque towns. Visitors can enjoy the luxurious beaches of Cannes, the picturesque town of Nice, or the historic city of Monaco.

The Loire Valley is another popular destination for tourists. This picturesque region is home to many châteaux, including the famous Château de Chambord. Visitors can take a tour of the châteaux, or simply stroll through the beautiful gardens.

Finally, the French Alps are a great destination for those looking to experience the great outdoors. The region is popular for skiing and snowboarding in the winter, and hiking and biking in the summer. Visitors can also enjoy the beautiful alpine scenery and the charming mountain villages.

France is a diverse country with many different sights and activities to offer. Whether you're interested in history, culture, or nature, there is something for everyone to enjoy. With a little planning and a sense of adventure, you're sure to have an unforgettable experience on your first trip to France.

Culture And Customs

Information on French culture, customs, and etiquette, including tips on how to navigate French social norms and avoid cultural faux pas.

France is a country rich in culture and history, known for its art, fashion, cuisine, and wine. Visitors to France will find a diverse range of customs and traditions that reflect its unique heritage.

One of the most iconic aspects of French culture is its art and architecture. From the famous paintings of the Louvre to the stunning Gothic architecture of Notre-Dame, there is no shortage of artistic treasures to discover in France. Visitors should also take the time to explore the country's many museums, galleries and exhibitions.

French cuisine is another highlight of the country's culture. From the classic dishes of French haute cuisine to the more rustic fare of the countryside, there is something for every taste. Some must-try dishes include escargots, ratatouille, bouillabaisse, and of course, the world-renowned French bread and pastries.

Wine is also a big part of French culture. The country is home to some of the world's most famous wine regions, including Bordeaux, Champagne, and Burgundy. Visitors can take a tour of one of the many vineyards or wine cellars, or simply enjoy a glass of wine with a meal.

Fashion is also an important part of French culture. The country is home to some of the world's most famous fashion designers and fashion houses, such as Chanel, Dior, and Yves Saint Laurent.

Visitors can take a stroll down the Champs-Élysées, where many of the world's top fashion brands have their flagship stores.

France is also known for its rich history and customs, which are reflected in the many festivals and celebrations that take place throughout the year. Some of the most famous include the Cannes Film Festival, the Tour de France, and the famous Bastille Day celebrations on July 14th. France is a country with a lot to offer visitors. Whether you're interested in art, history, fashion, or food, there is something for everyone to enjoy. With its stunning architecture, delicious cuisine, and rich culture, France is a destination that will leave a lasting impression on any first-time traveler.

Here are some **DO's** and **DON'Ts** when you are in France

DO's:

1. Greet people with a "Bonjour" or "Bonsoir" when entering a shop or restaurant, or when meeting someone.
2. Use "please" (s'il vous plaît) and "thank you" (merci) when making requests or expressing gratitude.
3. Use proper table manners when dining, such as keeping your hands visible on the table and not starting to eat until everyone has been served.
4. Dress nicely when visiting religious sites or upscale restaurants.

5. Learn a few basic French phrases, even if you're not fluent.
6. Respect French culture, traditions, and customs.

DON'Ts:

1. Don't be too loud or boisterous in public, as the French tend to be more reserved in public.
2. Don't enter a store or restaurant without first greeting the staff.
3. Don't speak loudly on your cell phone in public.
4. Don't tip as much as you would in the United States. A small amount (5-10%) is sufficient in most cases.
5. Don't be offended if a French person is direct or blunt in their communication, as this is seen as normal in French culture.

6. Don't ignore the smoking laws in France, it is illegal to smoke in enclosed public spaces such as restaurants and bars.

The most important thing is to be respectful of French culture and customs. This will help ensure that you have a pleasant and enjoyable trip to France.

Language

A guide to basic French phrases and vocabulary, including tips on how to communicate with locals and navigate common everyday situations.

The official language of France is French, which is spoken by the majority of the population. French is a Romance language, which means it is descended from Latin and is part of the same family as other

Romance languages such as Spanish, Italian, and Portuguese.

French is considered one of the most elegant and sophisticated languages in the world, and is known for its complex grammar and rich vocabulary. It is also the international language of diplomacy, as it is one of the official languages of many international organizations such as the United Nations and the European Union.

French is a phonetic language, which means that the words are pronounced as they are spelled. However, there are a few exceptions to this rule, such as the silent "h" and the nasal vowels. French also has a system of accent marks, known as "accent aigu" and "accent grave", which are used to indicate the pronunciation of certain letters.

One of the most challenging aspects of learning French is its complex grammar. French has many verb conjugations, tenses, and grammatical rules to master. However, the good news is that once you have a good grasp of the basic grammar, it becomes much easier to understand and use the language.

In terms of vocabulary, French has a lot of loanwords from other languages, particularly from Latin, Greek, and English. French also has a rich literary tradition, which has contributed to its vast vocabulary.

If you're planning to visit France, it's a good idea to learn at least some basic French before you go. Even if you don't become fluent, knowing a few key phrases will make it much easier to navigate the country and interact with the locals. There are many resources available to help you learn French, such as language classes, online tutorials, and language learning apps.

French is a beautiful and elegant language, spoken by millions of people around the world. It is a challenging language to learn, but with dedication and practice, anyone can master it. Whether you're planning a trip to France or simply want to expand your linguistic horizons, learning French is a rewarding experience.

Safety and health

Information on staying safe while traveling in France, including emergency contact information and tips on avoiding common travel hazards.

As with any foreign country, there are certain precautions that first-time travelers should take to stay safe and healthy.

Here are some tips to help you have a safe and enjoyable trip to France:

Get Vaccinated: Before you travel, make sure you are up-to-date on all of your vaccinations. This includes common vaccinations such as measles, mumps, and rubella, as well as any vaccinations recommended for travel to France, such as hepatitis A and B.

Pack Necessary Medications: If you have any chronic medical conditions or take any prescription medications, make sure to pack enough to last the duration of your trip. It's also a good idea to bring a copy of your prescriptions and a letter from your doctor explaining your condition and medications, in case you need to see a doctor in France.

Carry Travel Insurance: It's always a good idea to have travel insurance, especially when travelling to a foreign country. Make sure your insurance covers emergency medical treatment and evacuation, in case of an accident or illness.

Be aware of Food and Water Safety: The tap water in France is safe to drink, but it's always a good idea to be cautious when eating or drinking in unfamiliar places. Avoid tap water in rural areas, instead opt for bottled water. When it comes to food, stick to well-cooked and hot meals, and avoid street food if you're worried about hygiene.

Be aware of Scams: Like any tourist destination, there are scammers in France looking to take advantage of unsuspecting tourists. Be aware of common scams such as pickpocketing, fake police officers, and street vendors overcharging for goods. Keep your valuables close and be aware of your surroundings at all times.

Weather

Information on the climate in different parts of France, including average temperatures and precipitation levels, as well as tips on what to pack for different seasons.
France has a relatively moderate climate, with warm summers and cool winters. However, the weather can vary

considerably depending on the region you are visiting.

The northern and western parts of France, including Paris and the Loire Valley, have a temperate maritime climate. This means that summers are generally mild and winters can be quite cool, with occasional rain or drizzle throughout the year. Average temperatures in the summer are around 20°C (68°F), and in the winter they can drop to around 5°C (41°F).

The southern and eastern parts of France, including the French Riviera and the Alsace region, have a Mediterranean climate. This means that summers are generally hot and dry, with temperatures reaching up to 30°C (86°F) during the day. Winters are mild, with average temperatures around 10°C (50°F).

The French Alps have a mountain climate, with cold winters and cool summers. The temperature in the winter time drops to freezing point with heavy snowfall, making it a great destination for winter sports.

It's always a good idea to check the forecast before you leave and pack accordingly. It is also recommended to pack clothes that can be layered, so you can adjust to the weather conditions.

In-a-nutshell, France is a great destination to visit year-round, but the best time to visit will depend on your personal preferences and the specific destinations you plan to visit. It's always a good idea to check the forecast before you leave and pack accordingly.
The greatest time to visit France is during the seasons of spring, summer, and autumn. It implies that you may arrange a vacation between the months of April and

October. Overall, France delivers moderate weather throughout these months.

Are you visiting France as a couple?

Here are some cool places for lovers that you might want to check out.

Colmar: With architecture influenced by neighboring nation Germany, the tiny village of Colmar is just wonderful. You may wander along the river bank and observe the beautiful half-timbered buildings here.

Island of Aix: Bonding with your sweetheart is to take her away to the tranquility of the lovely Island of Aix. Here, you may discover the hidden alcoves and enjoy the pure white beaches.

Eze: Perched on a verdant mountain peak, the hamlet town of Eze is one of the most lovely tourist spots in France. Here, you may appreciate the amazing beauty of nature and wander through the small alleyways while being comfy with your sweetheart.

Etretat: Watching the seductive sunset on the cliffs of Etretat with your sweetheart is the type of romantic thought that is hard to duplicate. You can have some alone time while staring at the lovely colors in the sky.

Other interesting **places to visit in France**?
 You may ask, don't worry as this guide would work you through the best and attractive places you should or must visit before leaving France. And in no particular order they are as follows:-

Basilica of St. Michael

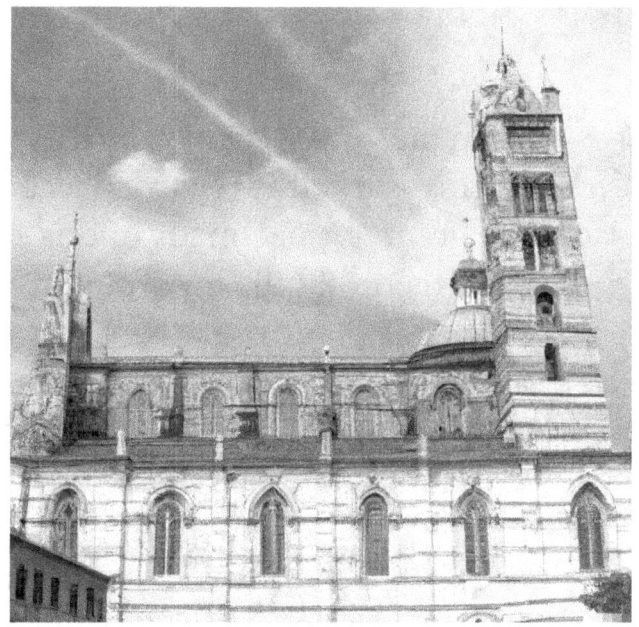

Photo of Basilica of Saint Michael

The Basilica of Saint Michael in France is a spectacular architectural marvel situated in the little hamlet of Saint-Michel-Chef-Chef, in the Loire-Atlantique region of France. The basilica is dedicated to the archangel Saint Michael, who is regarded as the patron saint of the town.

The basilica was erected in the Romanesque style in the 11th century, and it is regarded as one of the greatest specimens of this architectural type in France. The church is made of native tuff stone and contains a nave, two apses, and a transept, which are characteristic of the Romanesque architecture. The basilica is also embellished with exquisite sculptures, including a tympanum representing Saint Michael battling the devil, and a sequence of capitals depicting episodes from the Bible.

Inside the basilica, visitors may observe the gorgeous murals that grace the walls and ceilings, as well as the numerous complex carvings and sculptures that decorate the altar and pulpit. The basilica is also home to a number of noteworthy pieces of art, including a statue of Saint Michael by the famed French sculptor, Jean-Baptiste Pigalle.

The basilica is also recognized for its lovely gardens and park, which are placed surrounding the cathedral. The gardens are a popular area for people to rest and enjoy the magnificent surroundings. They are also home to a variety of sculptures and monuments, including a figure of Saint Michael by the French artist, Paul Landowski.

The Basilica of Saint Michael is a must-see attraction for anybody visiting the Loire-Atlantique area of France. The church's long history, spectacular architecture, and exquisite art make it one of the most significant cultural sites in the area.

The Basilica of Saint Michel is a remarkable architectural marvel situated in the little town of Saint-Michel-Chef-Chef, in the Loire-Atlantique region of France. Built in the Romanesque style in the 11th century, it is regarded as one of the greatest specimens of this architectural type in France. It is a notable cultural monument, with its rich history, spectacular architecture, and exquisite art. It is a must-see attraction for everyone visiting the Loire-Atlantique area of France.

Eiffel Tower

The Eiffel Tower, located in Paris, France, is one of the most iconic landmarks in the world. Standing at a towering height of 324 meters, it was built as the entrance arch to the 1889 World's Fair, and has since become a symbol of French culture and a major tourist attraction.

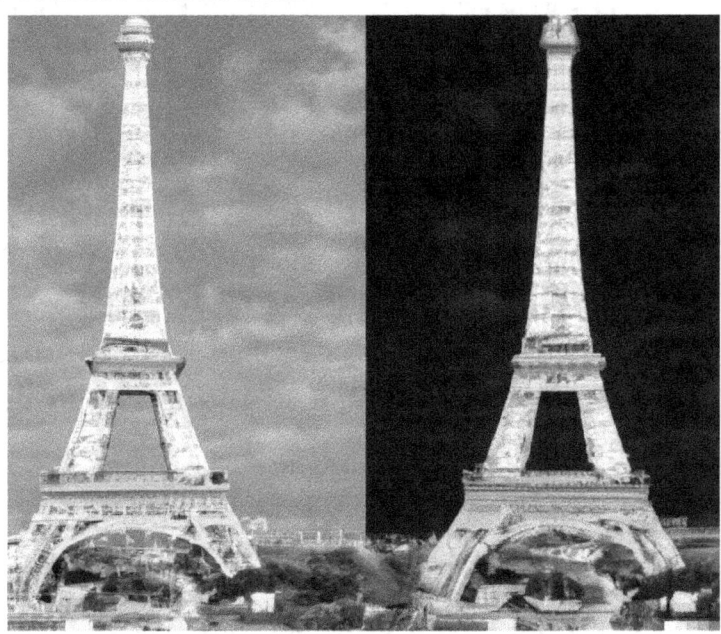

Eiffel Tower in the day and at night

The Eiffel Tower was designed by Gustave Eiffel, a French engineer, and was built in just over two years, from 1887 to 1889. At the time of its construction, it was the tallest man-made structure in the world, surpassing the Washington Monument in the United States.

The tower is made of iron and is divided into three levels, each with its own observation deck. The first level, at 57 meters, offers a view of the city of Paris and the surrounding area. The second level, at 115 meters, offers a view of the city and the surrounding countryside. The top level, at 276 meters, offers a panoramic view of the entire city and the surrounding area.

One of the most popular ways to experience the Eiffel Tower is by taking the elevator to the top. The elevator ride takes about one minute, and once you reach the top, you can take in the breathtaking views of Paris and its landmarks such as the Notre Dame Cathedral and the Arc de Triomphe.

Another popular way to experience the Eiffel Tower is by taking a guided tour. Guided tours are available in several languages, and they give you the opportunity to learn about the history and construction of the tower, as well as the interesting facts and stories behind it.

The Eiffel Tower is also a popular spot for romantic moments and proposals. Many couples come to the tower to propose or to celebrate their anniversary. The tower also offers a unique dining experience with a restaurant on the first level and a champagne bar on the second level.

In recent years, the Eiffel Tower has undergone several renovations and upgrades to improve safety and accessibility. The tower is now equipped with a state-of-the-art security system and a new elevator system to ensure the safety of visitors.

The Eiffel Tower is not just a landmark but a cultural icon of France, a must-see destination for tourists visiting Paris, and an enduring symbol of French engineering and architecture. The tower is a testament to the ingenuity and creativity of Gustave Eiffel and the many engineers and workers who helped bring his vision to life. It is a place where visitors can experience the history, culture, and beauty of Paris, and create memories that will last a lifetime.

Palais Garnier Opera House

The Palais Garnier Opera House, usually known as the Opéra Garnier or just the Garnier, is one of the most renowned and iconic opera houses in the world.

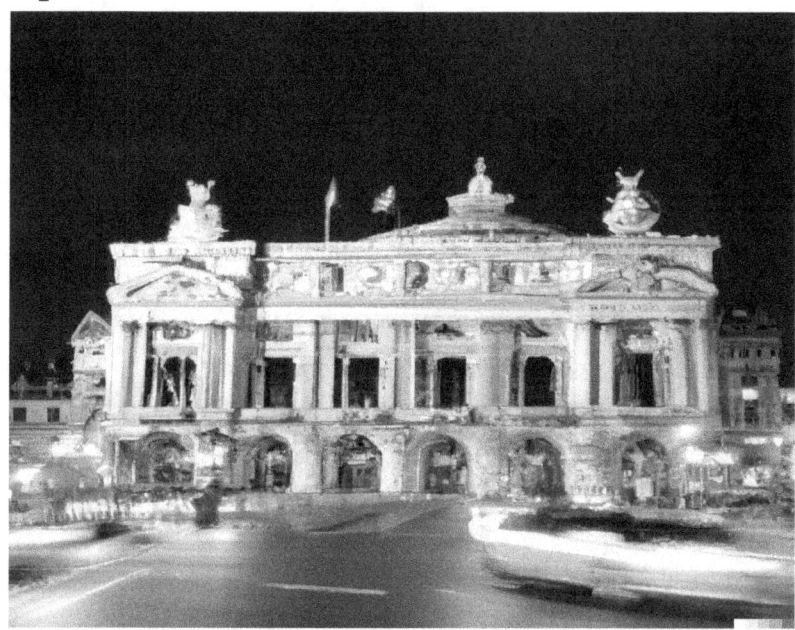

Night View of Palais Garnier Opera House

Located in Paris, France, the Garnier is a masterpiece of 19th century architecture and design, and has become a key cultural and historical monument for the city. The Garnier was erected between 1861 and 1875, and was designed by the famous French architect Charles Garnier. The structure is regarded to be one of the greatest specimens of the Second Empire style of architecture, which was prominent in France during the mid-19th century. The Garnier's enormous design is marked by its elaborate façade, huge marble staircase, and sumptuous interior ornamentation.

One of the most prominent elements of the Garnier is its vast entry hall, known as the Grand Foyer. This area is embellished with marble columns, elaborate frescoes, and a large chandelier that hangs from the ceiling. The Grand Foyer is also home to a number of famous pieces of art, including a painting by Pierre-Auguste Renoir and sculptures by Jean-Baptiste Carpeaux.

The Garnier's principal auditorium, or performance area, is known as the Salle de l'Opéra. This enormous hall is capable of seating over 1,900 people and is filled with intricate décor, including a big chandelier that hangs from the ceiling. The Salle de l'Opéra is also home to a number of famous pieces of art, including a painting by Jean-Léon Gérôme and sculptures by Auguste Rodin.

In addition to the main auditorium, the Garnier also has a number of additional performance venues, including a smaller theater known as the Salle de la Comédie-Française, as well as a number of practice rooms and dressing rooms. The Garnier also has a variety of additional public rooms, such as the Grand Foyer, which is commonly utilized for banquets and other events.

The Garnier has a rich history and has played a key part in the cultural life of Paris for almost a century. The structure has housed some of the most renowned and significant artists of the 19th and 20th centuries, including composer Richard Wagner, who conducted the debut of his opera "Tristan and Isolde" at the Garnier in 1882. The Garnier is especially noted for its relationship with the legendary French composer Claude Debussy, who launched his opera "Pelléas et Mélisande" at the Garnier in 1902.

Today, the Garnier is still a major cultural and historical monument in Paris and continues to stage performances of opera, ballet, and other events. The building is also available to the public and conducts tours, which let visitors explore the vast halls and public areas of the Garnier and learn more about its rich history and architecture.

The Palais Garnier Opera House is an architectural marvel of the 19th century, a huge edifice that was constructed by the famous architect Charles Garnier and inaugurated in 1875. The Garnier is a prominent cultural and historical site in Paris and continues to stage performances of opera, ballet, and other events. It is available to the public and provides tours, which let visitors explore the vast halls and public areas of the Garnier and learn more about its rich history and architecture.

Louvre Museum

The Louvre Museum, situated in Paris, France, is one of the most renowned and visited museums in the world. It is home to a rich collection of art and artifacts from ancient civilizations to the 21st century.

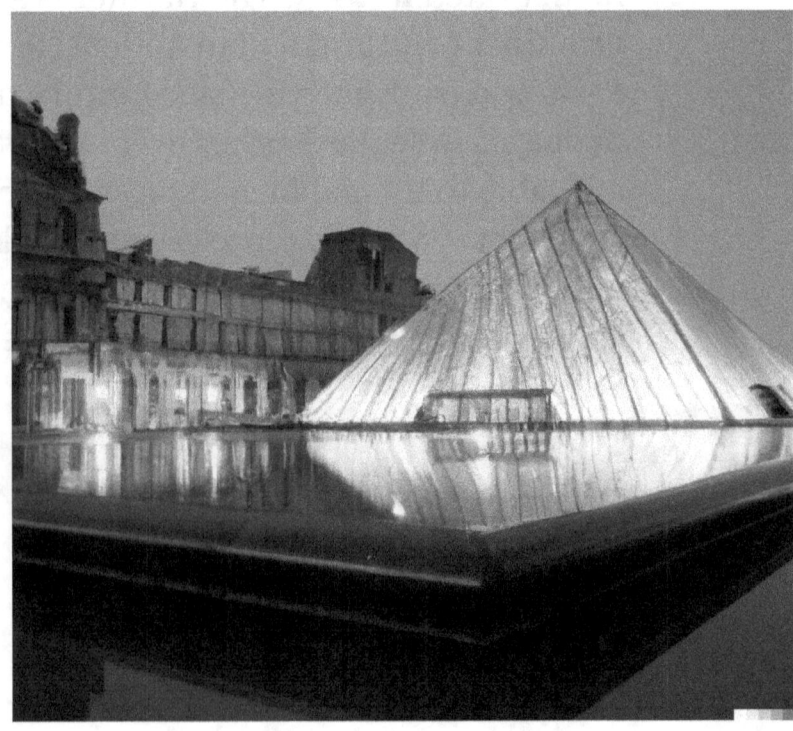

Louvre Museum

The Louvre was initially erected in the 12th century as a fortification, but was subsequently turned into a palace for French kings. In 1793, during the French Revolution, it was transformed into a public museum and has been available to the public ever since.

One of the most renowned works in the Louvre's collection is the Mona Lisa, painted by Leonardo da Vinci in the early 16th century. The artwork is noted for its enigmatic grin and is considered a masterpiece of Renaissance art. Other notable pieces at the Louvre include the Venus de Milo, a figure of the Greek goddess of love and beauty, and the Winged Victory of Samothrace, a marble sculpture from ancient Greece.

The Louvre also houses a huge collection of Egyptian antiquities, including the Great Sphinx of Tanis and the Seated Scribe. The collection of Islamic art is one of the most comprehensive in the world, comprising pieces from the 8th to the 19th century. The Louvre's collection of decorative arts is very significant and includes furniture, pottery, and other things from the Middle Ages to the current age.

The Louvre is a huge museum, with over 380,000 items divided over eight curatorial divisions. It might be daunting to view everything in one visit, therefore it is important to prepare ahead and choose which parts you would want to see. The museum provides a range of tours, both guided and self-directed, to assist visitors browse the collection.

The Louvre is a must-see site for art enthusiasts and history fans. Its large collection and historical importance make it one of the most significant and recognizable museums in the world.

The Louvre is open every day except Tuesday. It is closed on January 1, May 1, and December 25. Visitors may buy tickets online in advance to bypass the lineups.

Notre Dame Cathedral

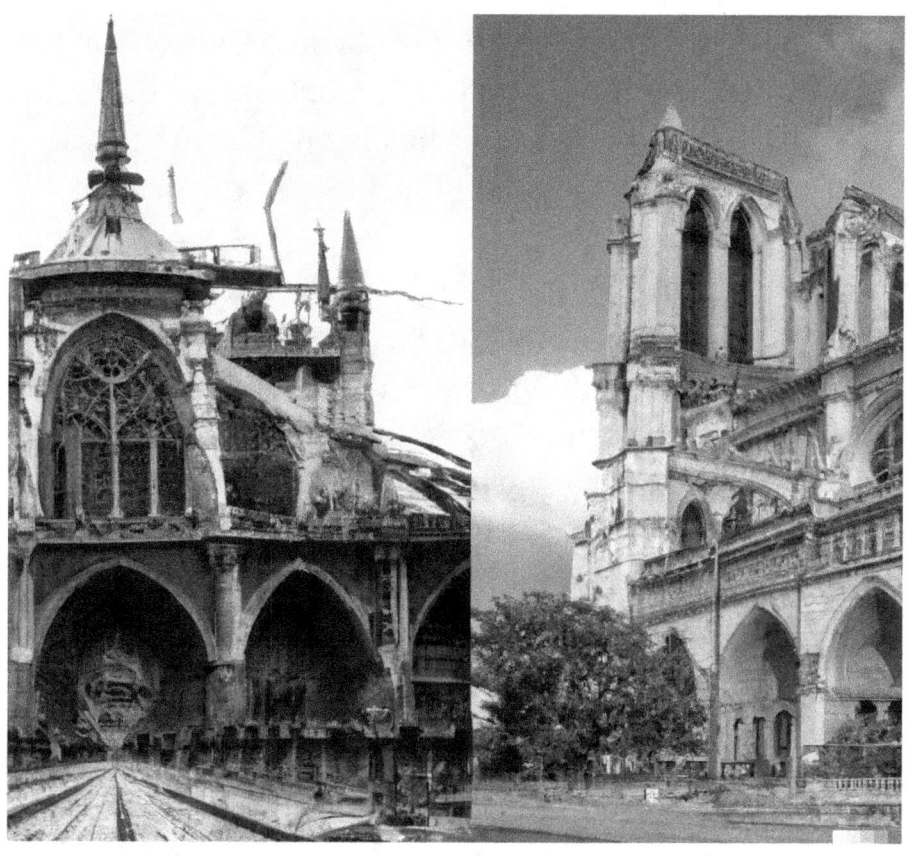

The Notre Dame Cathedral after the fire and before the fire incident.

Notre Dame Cathedral, situated in the centre of Paris, France, is one of the most famous and identifiable structures in the world. The cathedral, which dates back to the 12th century, is a masterpiece of Gothic architecture and has been classified as a UNESCO World Heritage Site.

Notre Dame, which translates as "Our Lady" in English, was erected on the site of an ancient church that had been devoted to the Virgin Mary. Construction of the cathedral started in 1163 under the guidance of Bishop Maurice de Sully and took approximately 200 years to finish. The cathedral was consecrated in 1345.

The outside of Notre Dame is embellished with elaborate carvings and sculptures, including three enormous rose windows and two towers, which reach a height of almost 200 feet. The western front of the cathedral has the famed gargoyles, which were erected in the 13th century to function as drainage spouts and as a method to fend off bad spirits.

Inside, the cathedral is just as stunning, with its ribbed ceilings, pointed arches, and vivid stained glass windows. The wide nave, which is studded with chapels, is especially stunning, and the high altar is graced with a lovely figure of the Virgin Mary.

Notre Dame has played a vital part in French history and culture. It has been the location of numerous notable events, notably the crowning of Napoleon Bonaparte as Emperor of France in 1804. The cathedral also served as the inspiration for Victor Hugo's classic book, "The Hunchback of Notre Dame."

In April 2019, a massive fire broke out in the cathedral which extensively damaged the roof and caused the fall of the spire. The French government and private benefactors have offered millions of dollars to restore the cathedral to its former splendor and repair the damage inflicted by the fire. The French government wants to reopen the church to the public in 2024.

Notre Dame Cathedral is a real architectural marvel and a symbol of the rich history and culture of France. It continues to be one of the most frequented tourist sites in Paris, with millions of people each year.

Palace Of Versaille

The Palace of Versailles, situated in the Île-de-France region of France, is a beautiful example of French Baroque architecture. Built in the 17th century by King Louis XIV, the palace served as the royal home and seat of political authority for the French monarchy until the French Revolution in 1789.

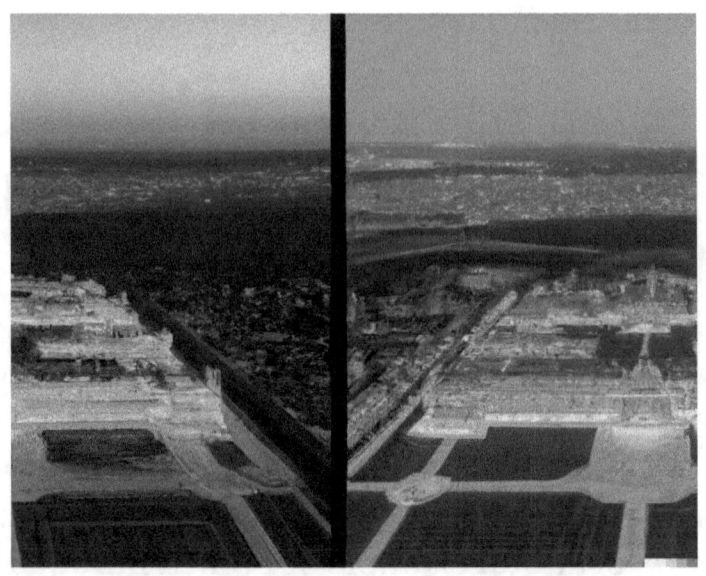

A glimpse of Palace Of Versaille day and night image

The castle is surrounded by gorgeous gardens, which were built by André Le Nôtre and are regarded as some of the most beautiful in the world. The gardens showcase a variety of sculpted hedges, elaborate fountains, and carefully groomed grass. Visitors may take a walk around the gardens, which encompass over 800 hectares, and enjoy the gorgeous surroundings.

The palace itself is a masterwork of architecture and is known for its wealth and majesty. The Hall of Mirrors, one of the palace's most renowned chambers, is a vast hall that is adorned with 17 mirror-clad arches, which reflect the light from the massive windows, producing a brilliant show.

The palace is also home to a number of other remarkable chambers, including the Royal Chapel, the King's Bedchamber, and the Queen's Apartments. The castle also holds a significant art collection, which includes works by some of the most prominent painters of the period, including Rubens, Van Dyck, and Veronese.

Today, the Palace of Versailles is a major tourist site, receiving millions of tourists each year. It is available to the public and provides tours of the palace and grounds, as well as special exhibits and activities. Visitors may also enjoy a range of food options and retail alternatives inside the royal grounds.

The Palace of Versailles is not just an architectural marvel but also a symbol of the French monarchy, its history and its majesty. It is a must-see sight for everyone interested in French history and culture.

Mont Saint-Michel

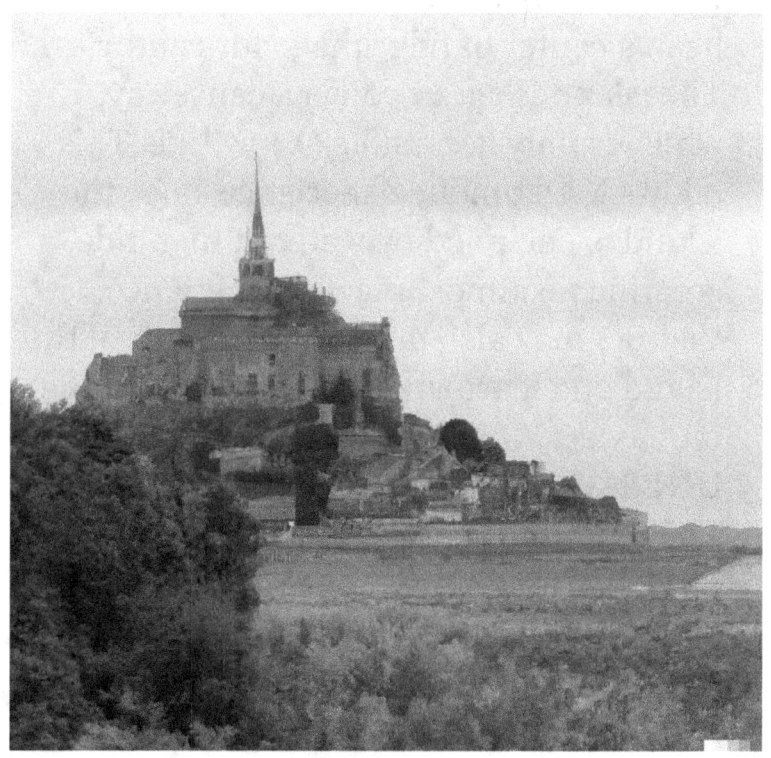

Image view of Mont Saint Michel

Mont Saint-Michel is a tiny island situated off the coast of Normandy, France. It is noted for its gorgeous medieval architecture and rich history. The island is home to a Benedictine monastery, which was founded in the 8th century and has been a center of pilgrimage for centuries. The island is accessed via a causeway, which is only accessible at low tide. This allows for a unique experience since the island is encircled by water at high tide, creating an almost magical ambiance. Visitors may also take a guided tour of the island and learn about its history and the monastery, which has been named a UNESCO World Heritage site.

The monastery is the principal attraction of Mont Saint-Michel, and tourists may explore the numerous halls and chapels inside the abbey. The construction is a blend of Gothic and Romanesque styles, and the abbey is embellished with beautiful carvings and paintings. The monastery also features a museum that shows the history of the island and the

abbey, featuring artifacts and manuscripts going back to the 8th century.
Mont Saint-Michel is also home to a tiny settlement, which is situated at the foot of the island. The community is home to a few restaurants, stores, and motels. Visitors may also visit the walls of the settlement, which give wonderful views of the island and the surrounding water.

In addition to its history and architecture, Mont Saint-Michel is also noted for its natural beauty. The island is home to a variety of species, including seagulls, bats, and even seals. Visitors may also explore the various hiking routes that run around the island, affording spectacular views of the bay and the abbey.
The island provides a unique combination of history, architecture, and natural beauty that is really remarkable. With its majestic ancient abbey and lovely hamlet, Mont

Saint-Michel is a place that will make a lasting impact on everyone who comes.

Disneyland Paris

Disneyland Paris, commonly known as Euro Disney, is a theme park resort situated in Marne-la-Vallée, a new town located around 20 miles east of the heart of Paris, France.

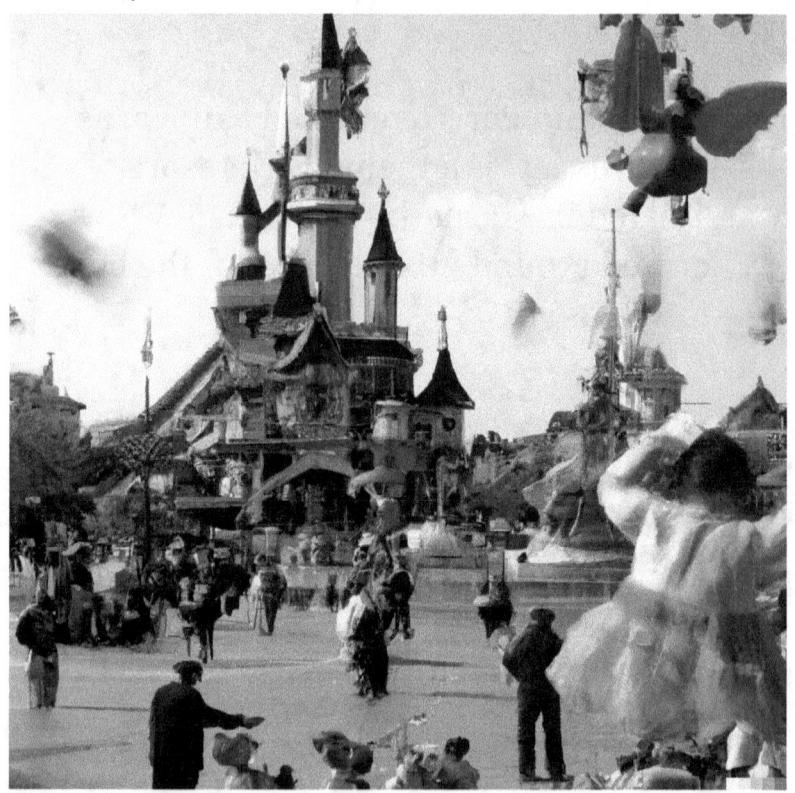

A view of Disneyland Paris

The resort debuted on April 12, 1992 and is the second Disney park to open outside of the United States, following Tokyo Disney Resort.

The resort is made up of two theme parks: Disneyland Park and Walt Disney Studios Park. Disneyland Park is the original park and is separated into five themed lands: Main Street, U.S.A., Adventureland, Frontierland, Fantasyland, and Discoveryland. Walt Disney Studios Park, which opened in 2002, is organized into four production zones: Front Lot, Toon Studio, Production Courtyard, and Backlot. The Disneyland Park is home to famous Disney attractions such as "It's a Small World", "Pirates of the Caribbean", and "Space Mountain".

The park also boasts various events and parades, including the "Disney Magic on Parade" and the "Disney Dreams" evening spectacular. The Walt Disney Studios Park contains attractions and shows that take audiences behind the scenes of movie creation and animation, including "Crush's

Coaster", "The Twilight Zone Tower of Terror", and "Cinemagique".
In addition to the two theme parks, Disneyland Paris also contains Disney Village, an eating and entertainment center, and many Disney-owned hotels, including Disney's Hotel New York, Disney's Newport Bay Club, and Disney's Sequoia Lodge.

Disneyland Paris is a must-visit site for Disney enthusiasts and families. With its unique combination of traditional Disney attractions and innovative experiences, it provides something for everyone. While visiting the park, one may take advantage of the various food and shopping opportunities, as well as the Disney-owned hotels, which provide pleasant rooms and convenient access to the parks.

Seine Cruise

The Seine Cruise in France is a popular tourist activity that offers a unique and picturesque way to explore the city of Paris.

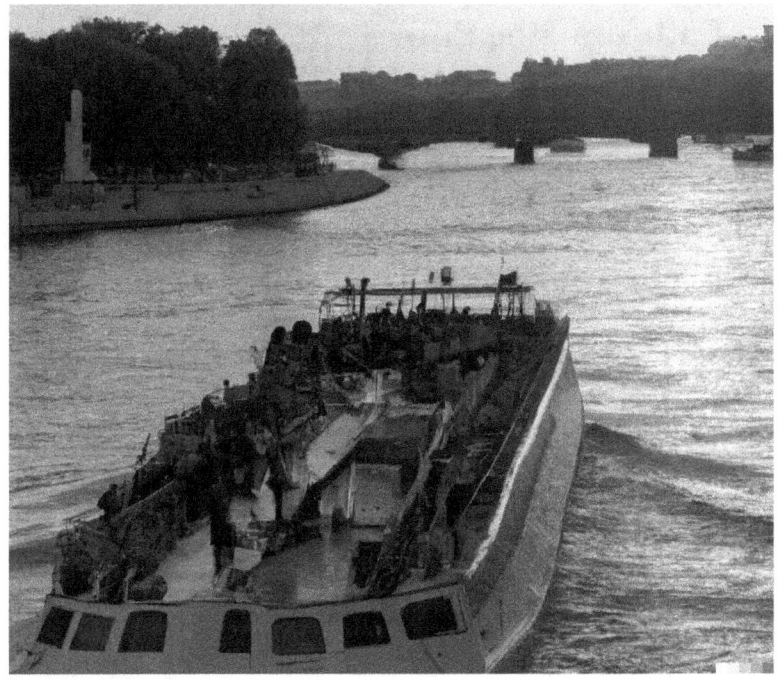

Seine CruiseLa sunset view

The river Seine runs through the heart of Paris and offers a different perspective of the city's famous landmarks and monuments.

The cruise typically lasts for about an hour and takes passengers past some of Paris' most iconic sights, including Notre-Dame Cathedral, the Eiffel Tower, the Louvre Museum, and the Musée d'Orsay. The boats used for the cruise are specially designed to provide a comfortable and enjoyable experience, with large windows to allow for unobstructed views of the city.

One of the best ways to experience a Seine Cruise is at night when the city is lit up, offering a magical and romantic atmosphere. The Eiffel Tower, in particular, is a stunning sight as it sparkles with thousands of lights.

In addition to the stunning views, many Seine Cruise boats also offer on-board dining and entertainment,making it a perfect option for a special occasion or romantic evening out. Some boats even have glass-enclosed decks for a panoramic view of the city.

A Seine Cruise is a must-do activity for any traveler visiting Paris. The cruise offers a unique and enjoyable way to explore the city, providing a perspective of Paris that cannot be found on foot or by car. Whether you're a first-time visitor or a seasoned traveler, a Seine Cruise is a memorable experience that should not be missed.

 Seine Cruise is a great way to see the city of Paris, with its famous landmarks and monuments, while enjoying a comfortable and enjoyable experience. It's a perfect activity for everyone, whether you're a first-time visitor or a seasoned traveler, and it's definitely worth putting on your bucket list while you're in Paris.

La Cote des Basques

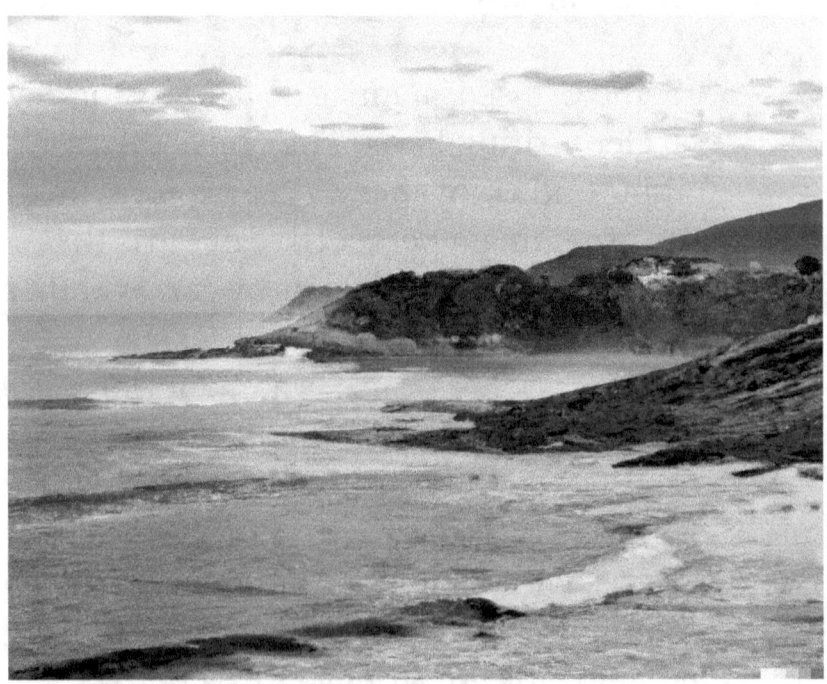

Image of La Cote des Basques coast

La Cote des Basques is a magnificent length of coastline situated in the southwestern area of France. The region is noted for its stunning beaches, lovely coastal villages, and world-renowned surf areas.

One of the most popular beaches in La Côte des Basques is the Plage de la Côte des Basques, which is situated in the town of Biarritz. This beach is popular among surfers, since the waves here may reach up to six feet in height. In addition to surfing, the beach also provides a range of other activities such as swimming, sunbathing, and beach volleyball.

Another renowned place in La Cote des Basques is the town of Saint-Jean-de-Luz. This lovely hamlet is noted for its tiny alleys, colorful buildings, and wonderful seafood. Visitors may also enjoy a range of water activities such as sailing and windsurfing, or take a boat ride to visit the adjacent cliffs and sea caves.

In addition to its natural beauty, La Cote des Basques also boasts a rich cultural legacy. The region has been a favorite destination for artists and writers for many years, and it is home to various museums and art galleries that highlight the work of local and international artists.

If you're searching for a calm beach holiday or an action-packed surf excursion, La Cote des Basques is the right spot. Whether you're a seasoned surfer or a first-time tourist, you're bound to find something that appeals to you in this picturesque corner of France.

Arc De Triomphe

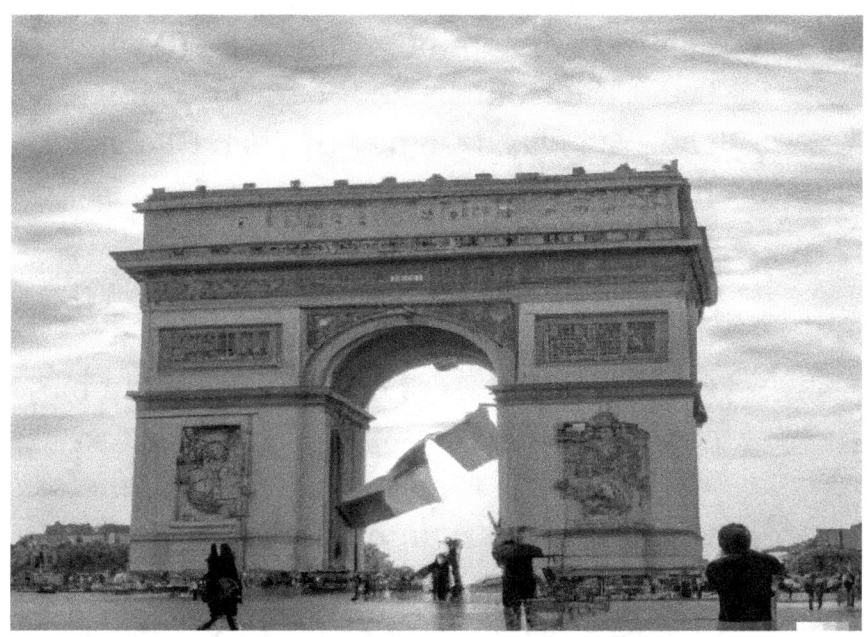

A view of the Arc De Triomphe

The Arc de Triomphe is one of the most prominent structures in Paris, France. It lies in the heart of the Place Charles de Gaulle, near the western end of the Champs-Élysées, and is the biggest triumphal arch in the world.

The Arc de Triomphe was commissioned by Napoleon Bonaparte in 1806 to celebrate his military achievements and to thank the troops who fought for France. The arch was designed by Jean Chalgrin and took 30 years to complete. It was ultimately finished in 1836, decades after Napoleon's death.

The Arc de Triomphe rises at a height of 50 meters (164 feet) and is 45 meters (148 feet) broad. It is embellished with reliefs and sculptures commemorating major events in French history, such as the Battle of Austerlitz and the Battle of Waterloo. The most renowned sculpture atop the Arc de Triomphe is the "Statue of the Republic," which sits at the summit of the arch. The Arc de Triomphe is also the location of the Tomb of the Unknown Soldier, which commemorates the troops who perished in World War I. The grave is positioned beneath the arch and is marked by an everlasting flame. Each evening at 6:30 pm, a ceremony is done in which a soldier from the French army places a wreath at the grave and the flame is rekindled.

Visitors may climb to the top of the Arc de Triomphe to experience panoramic views of Paris. The hike is tough, but it is worth it for the beautiful views over the city. The arch is also a popular site for visitors to snap photographs and to view the steady flow of traffic around the roundabout.

The Arc de Triomphe is a symbol of French pride and a must-see for anybody visiting Paris. It is a marvel of French architecture and a testimony to the country's rich past.

Grand Théâtre de Bordeaux

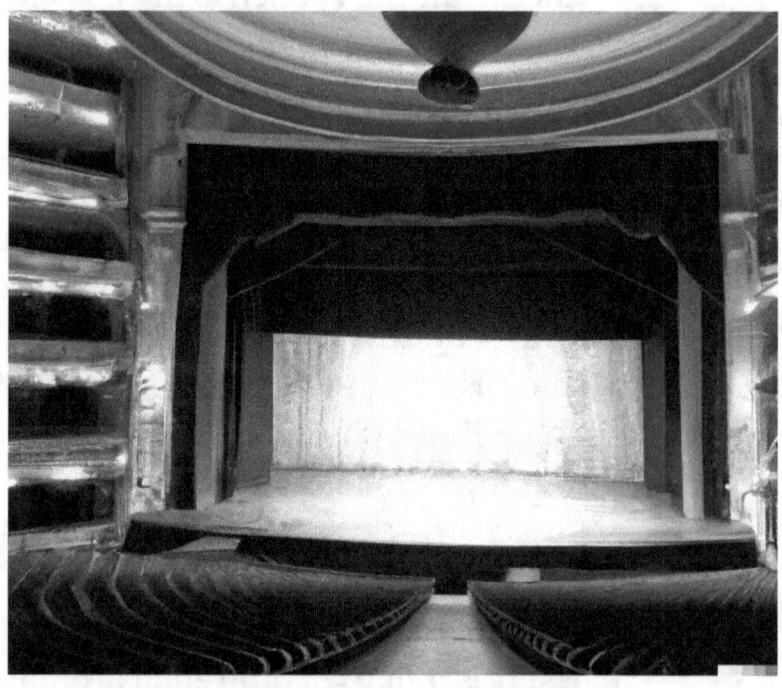

Stage view of the Grand Théâtre de Bordeaux

The Grand Théâtre de Bordeaux, popularly known as the Bordeaux Opera Theatre, is a magnificent and historic opera house situated in the center of the city of

Bordeaux, France. Built in the late 18th century, the Grand Théâtre de Bordeaux is regarded to be one of the most prominent specimens of French neoclassical architecture.

The opera theater was created by the architect Victor Louis, who was commissioned to build the Grand Théâtre de Bordeaux by the Duke of Richelieu. The building of the opera house started in 1773 and was finished in 1780. The Large Théâtre de Bordeaux boasts a grand marble staircase, exquisite murals, and elaborate chandeliers, all of which add to its grand and luxurious look.

The Grand Théâtre de Bordeaux has a seating capacity of 1,200 and is home to the Opéra National de Bordeaux, which performs a diverse selection of operas, ballets, and concerts throughout the year. The theater has hosted many great artists and performances, including the works of the famed French composer Georges Bizet, whose opera "Carmen" debuted at the Grand Théâtre de Bordeaux in 1875.

In addition to presenting concerts, the Grand Théâtre de Bordeaux is also available to the public for tours. Visitors may tour the theater's stunning architecture and learn about its history and importance to the city of Bordeaux. The theater also holds special events and exhibits throughout the year.

The Grand Théâtre de Bordeaux is not only an architectural wonder but also a cultural landmark of the city of Bordeaux. It continues to be a symbol of the city's rich cultural legacy and draws people from all over the globe. Its beautiful architecture, historical importance, and current cultural programming make it a must-see attraction for everyone visiting **Bordeaux.**

Promenade des Anglais

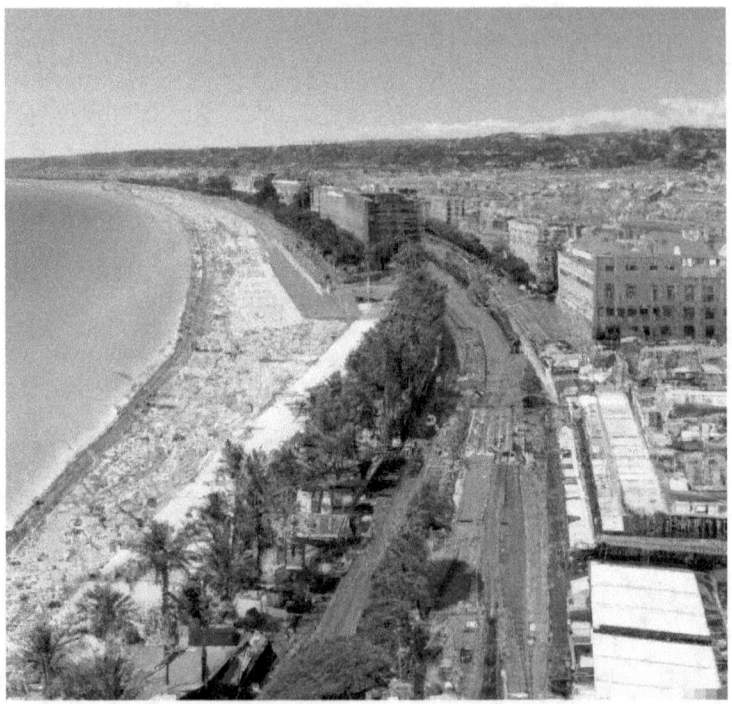

Image of Promenade des Anglais

The Promenade des Anglais, or "Walkway of the English," is a renowned beach promenade situated in the city of Nice,

France. It spans about 7 kilometers along the Mediterranean Sea and is a popular attraction for both residents and visitors.

The promenade was established in the early 1800s, during a period when the English upper class was spending their winters in the pleasant temperature of the French Riviera. They would take lengthy walks by the shore, and so the promenade was named in their honor.

Today, the Promenade des Anglais is a lively area packed with stores, restaurants, and cafés. It is a popular area for running, bicycling, and rollerblading, and is also home to multiple beaches. The most renowned of them is the Plage Beau Rivage, which was visited by the likes of F. Scott Fitzgerald and Ernest Hemingway in the 1920s and 30s.

One of the most recognizable sights along the promenade is the Negresco Hotel, which was erected in 1913 and is recognized for its elaborate architecture and luxury services. The hotel has played home to many renowned visitors throughout the years, including Winston Churchill and Charles de Gaulle.

The promenade is also noted for its lovely gardens, such as the Albert 1st Gardens and the Massena Gardens, which give a calm getaway from the rush and bustle of the city. The gardens are home to a variety of plants and flowers, and are a popular area for picnics and leisure.

Overall, the Promenade des Anglais is a must-see attraction for anybody visiting Nice. It provides a unique combination of history, culture, and natural beauty, and is the ideal site to take in the spectacular Mediterranean Sea views.

Castle Hill

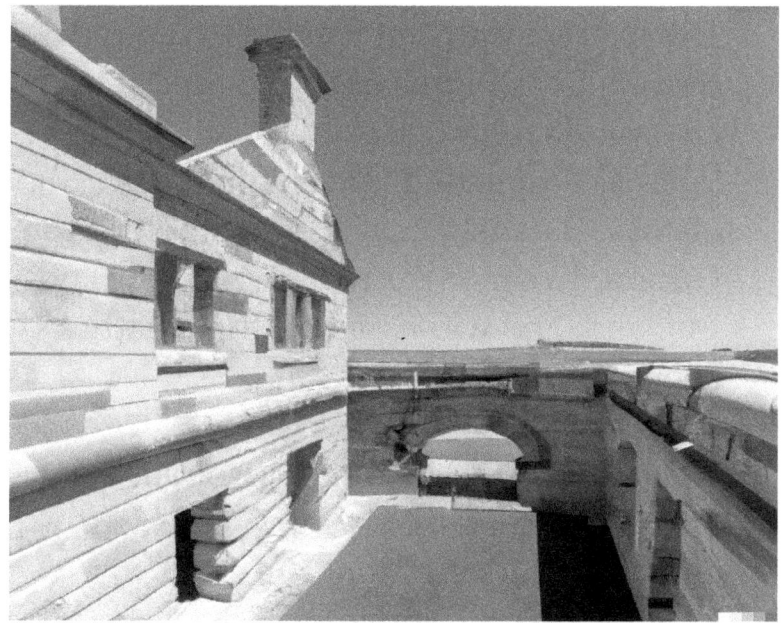

An image of Castle hill

Castle Hill, also known as Château de Castelnaud, is a medieval castle situated in the Dordogne area of France. The castle lies high on a hill above the Dordogne River and provides excellent views of the surrounding area.

The fortress was first erected in the 12th century by the lords of Beynac and was afterwards rebuilt and improved by the lords of Castelnaud. Throughout its history, the castle played a vital role in the Hundred Years' War between France and England, and witnessed multiple battles and sieges.

Today, the castle is available to tourists and gives a look into medieval life and battle. Visitors may tour the castle's various turrets, ramparts, and courtyards, and view the collection of medieval weaponry and armor on exhibit. The castle also has a museum that exhibits a variety of objects from the castle's history, including ceramics, textiles, and papers.

One of the delights of a visit to Castle Hill is the chance to see a medieval siege demonstration. Visitors may witness as a team of professional archers, crossbowmen, and trebuchet operators fire at the castle walls, recreating the sights and sounds of a medieval siege.

In addition to the castle itself, there are also various more attractions in the region. The town of Castelnaud-la-Chapelle, situated right below the castle, is a lovely medieval village that is home to various restaurants and stores. Visitors may also take a boat trip of the Dordogne River or go hiking in the nearby region.

Overall, Castle Hill is a must-see location for history fans and anybody interested in medieval castles. Its strategic position and rich history make it one of the most significant castles in the Dordogne area, and its gorgeous environment and diversity of activities make it a perfect destination for a day trip or a longer stay.

Place Garibaldi

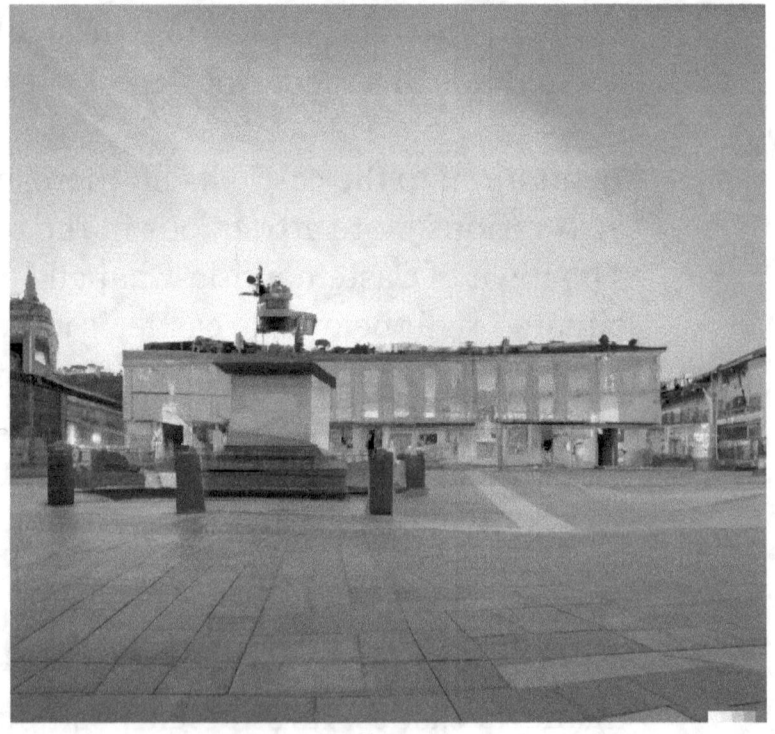

Sunset view of the Place Garibaldi

Place Garibaldi is a public area situated in the city of Nice, on the French Riviera. The plaza is named after the Italian commander and politician, Giuseppe Garibaldi, who played a crucial part in the unification of Italy in the 19th century.

The area is situated in the centre of Nice's Old Town and is surrounded by a variety of shops, restaurants, and cafés. One of the most famous aspects of the area is the statue of Garibaldi, which sits in the middle and serves as a popular gathering point for residents and visitors alike.

Place Garibaldi is also renowned for its active nightlife, with a multitude of pubs and clubs situated in the neighboring streets. The area is also a famous site for street performers, who amuse visitors with music, dancing, and acrobatic displays.

In addition to its bustling ambiance, Place Garibaldi is also home to a variety of historical and cultural sites. The neighboring Musée d'Art Moderne et d'Art Contemporain, for example, shows a broad spectrum of contemporary art by local and international artists. The neighboring Palais Lascaris, a 17th-century palace, is well worth a visit, since it holds a collection of ancient musical instruments and other historical relics.

Place Garibaldi is a must-see attraction for anybody visiting Nice. With its bustling atmosphere, historical and cultural attractions, and stunning Mediterranean environment, it provides something for everyone. Whether you're wanting to take in the sights and sounds of the city, enjoy a night out on the town, or learn about the history and culture of the area, Location Garibaldi is the right place to start.

Pont Alexandre III

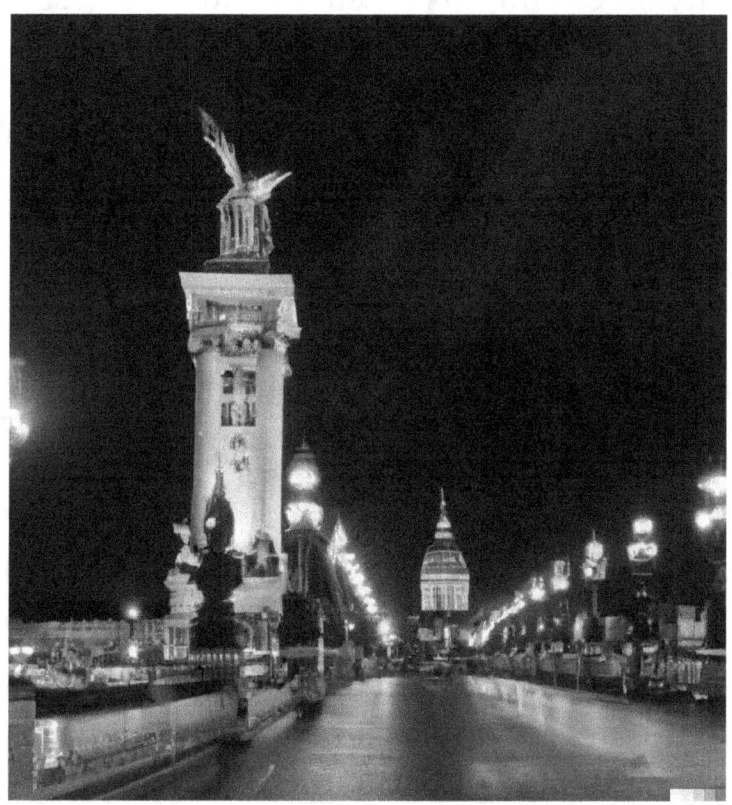

The night view of Pont Alexandre III

The Pont Alexandre III is a magnificent bridge situated in the middle of Paris,

France. Spanning the Seine River, the bridge links the Champs-Élysées to the Invalides and was erected in honor of Tsar Alexander III of Russia. It is regarded as one of the most exquisite and ornate bridges in Paris and is a favorite location for visitors and residents alike.

Designed by the architects Joseph Cassien-Bernard and Gaston Cousin, the Pont Alexandre III was erected between 1896 and 1900. The bridge is composed of steel and is embellished with intricate ornaments made of gilded bronze, featuring four winged horses, four nymphs, and four winged victors. The bridge also has four stone piers with sculptures of different people, including the French Republic and the Russian Empire.

The Pont Alexandre III is also notable for its exquisite lampposts and lamps. The lampposts are constructed of gilded bronze and depict complex motifs of winged horses, nymphs, and victorious figures. The streetlights are similarly constructed of gilded bronze and feature a distinctive motif of a winged horse.

One of the most recognizable characteristics of the Pont Alexandre III is the two colossal sculptures positioned at the entrance of the bridge. The sculptures feature two individuals, one representing the French Republic and the other representing the Russian Empire. The sculptures are made of bronze and are a symbol of the friendship and solidarity between the two nations.

The Pont Alexandre III is a popular site for visitors and residents alike. It provides beautiful views of the Seine River, the Eiffel Tower, and the Invalides. The bridge is also a favorite area for photographers and is a popular setting for wedding and engagement shots.

The Pont Alexandre III is a gorgeous and elegant bridge situated in the middle of Paris, France. It is a symbol of the friendship and cooperation between the French Republic and the Russian Empire and is a popular location for visitors and residents alike. The bridge provides breathtaking views of the Seine River and the Eiffel Tower and is a must-see for anybody visiting Paris.

Museum of Fine Arts of Lyon

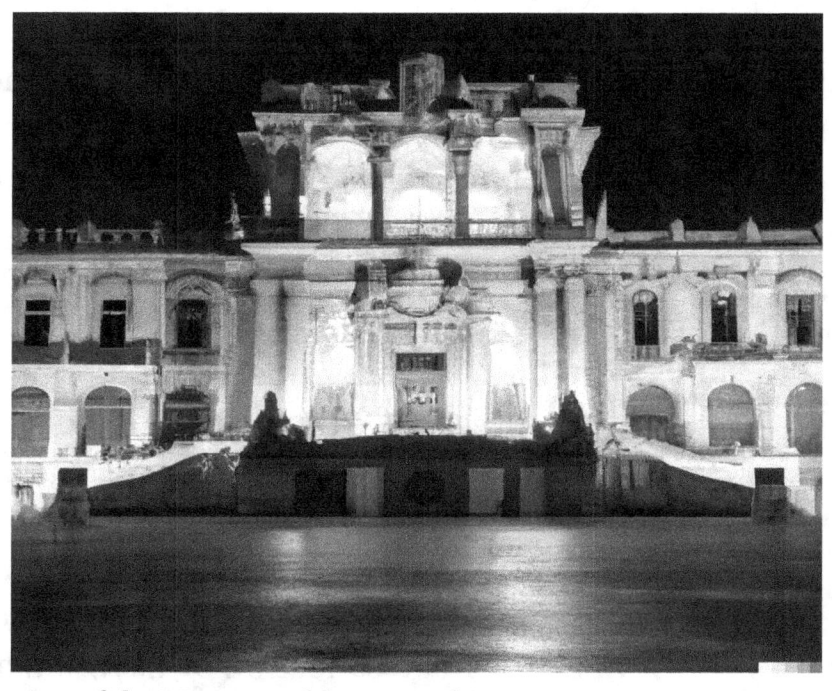

A night view of the Museum of fine arts of Lyon

The Museum of Fine Arts of Lyon, commonly known as the Musée des Beaux-Arts de Lyon, is a museum situated in Lyon, France. Founded in 1803, the museum is noted for its large collection of artworks from ancient to current times.

The museum's collection contains pieces from ancient Egypt, Greece, and Rome, as well as works from the Middle Ages and the Renaissance. The museum also boasts a rich collection of European art from the 17th to the 19th century, including works by prominent painters such as Rubens, Rembrandt, and Monet. In addition, the museum houses a collection of modern art, including pieces by Picasso and Warhol.

One of the centerpieces of the museum is the collection of ancient art. The museum houses a huge collection of Egyptian art, including sculptures, sarcophagi, and other relics from ancient Egypt. The museum also houses a collection of Greek and Roman art, including sculptures, vases, and other artifacts from ancient Greece and Rome.

Another attraction of the museum is the collection of European art. The museum features a substantial collection of art from the 17th to the 19th century, including works by prominent painters such as Rubens, Rembrandt, and Monet. The museum also features a collection of modern art, including pieces by Picasso and Warhol.

The Museum of Fine Arts of Lyon also holds a variety of temporary exhibits throughout the year, displaying work from many historical periods and places. These exhibits give visitors the chance to view a broad range of art, and to learn more about the artists and the historical environment in which the work was produced.

The museum is set in a lovely edifice in the centre of Lyon, which was erected in 1803 to hold the collection. The building has had various modifications over the years, and now it is a contemporary and large structure that is well-suited to the presentation of the museum's collection. The museum also features a library and a research center, which are open to academics and researchers who seek to examine the museum's collection.

The Museum of Fine Arts of Lyon is a must-see attraction for art aficionados visiting Lyon. With its wide collection of art from ancient to current times, temporary exhibits and stunning buildings, it is a terrific destination to spend a day discovering the world of art. And given its position in the center of Lyon, it is conveniently accessible for tourists to the city.

Notre-Dame de la Garde

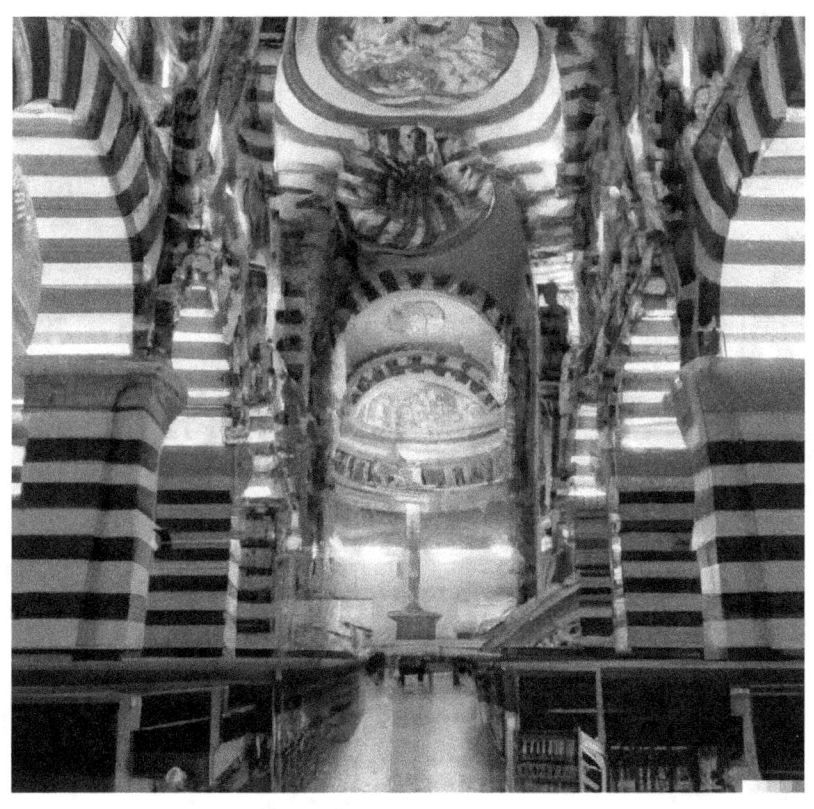

Inside Notre-Dame de la Garde.

Notre-Dame de la Garde, often known as "Our Lady of the Guard," is a notable church situated in the city of Marseille, France. The basilica lies on a hill in the southern side of the city, affording beautiful views of the surrounding area.

The basilica was erected in the 1850s in the Romano-Byzantine architectural style, and its design was significantly inspired by the churches and cathedrals found in the Middle East. The outside of the basilica contains a variety of elaborate embellishments, including bright mosaics, elegant sculptures, and precise carvings.

The most prominent feature of Notre-Dame de la Garde is its huge, golden statue of the Virgin Mary, which sits at the top of the basilica's bell tower. The monument is visible from many sections of the city and has become a symbol of Marseille. Visitors may climb the steps to the top of the bell tower to get a closer look at the monument and enjoy panoramic views of the city.

Inside, the basilica is equally as stunning as the façade. The main altar is embellished with elaborate carvings, and the walls are covered with stunning murals. The basilica also has various chapels, each with its own distinctive decorations and artwork.

Notre-Dame de la Garde is more than simply a religious institution, it is a symbol of Marseille's history and culture. The basilica has played an essential part in the city's history, acting as a beacon of hope for seafarers and a haven of shelter for the citizens of Marseille during times of conflict.

The church is also a popular location for visitors visiting Marseille. Many tourists come to witness the basilica's spectacular architecture, take in the views from the top of the bell tower, and visit the tiny museum situated within. The museum shows various historical items and artwork, including a collection of religious sculptures, paintings and other artworks.

Notre-Dame de la Garde is a must-see attraction for anybody visiting Marseille. The basilica's distinctive design, rich history, and magnificent vistas make it an attraction that should not be missed. Whether you are a history enthusiast, an art lover, or just seeking for a lovely spot to visit, Notre-Dame de la Garde is guaranteed to amaze.

Abbey of Saint-Victor de Marseille

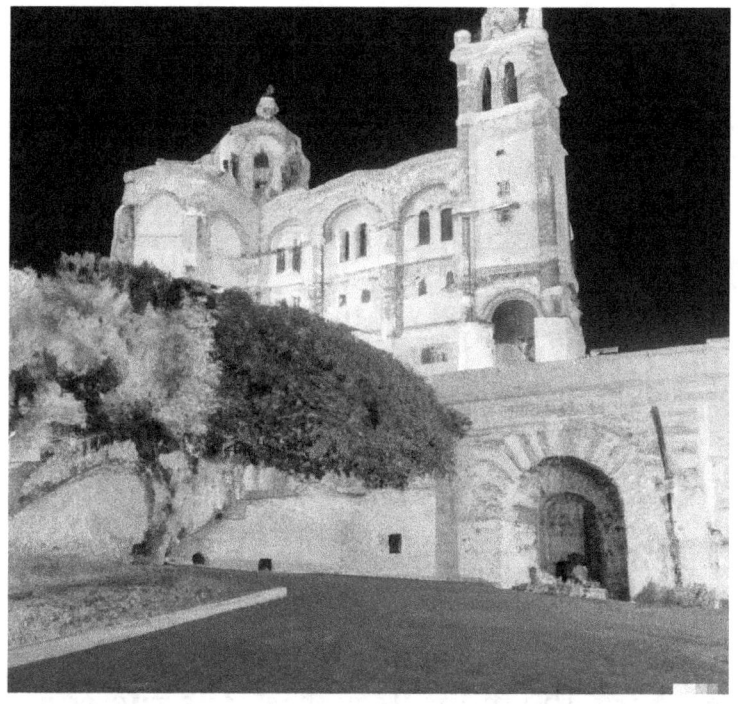

The outside of Abbey of Saint-Victor de Marseille at night

The Abbey of Saint-Victor de Marseille is a medieval church and monastery situated in the city of Marseille, France. Founded in the 4th century, it is one of the oldest Christian monasteries in the world and has a rich history steeped in religious and cultural importance.

The monastery was initially built by John Cassian, a Christian monk and theologian, in the 4th century. Cassian came to Marseille from Egypt and founded a monastic community on the location of the existing monastery. The community swiftly flourished and became an important center for Christian instruction and worship.

Throughout its history, the abbey has undergone various important modifications and extensions. In the 12th century, the monastery was constructed in the Romanesque style, and in the 18th century, it was enlarged and remodeled in the Baroque style. The abbey now has a blend of architectural styles, reflecting its long and diverse past.

One of the most prominent aspects of the abbey is its gorgeous cloister, which dates back to the 12th century. The cloister is a tranquil and private garden area encircled by arched galleries, and it is a favorite location for tourists to take a walk and observe the architecture.

The abbey also boasts a number of other noteworthy architectural and historical structures, including the Crypt of Saint Victor, which is thought to be the earliest Christian monument in Marseille, and the Treasury, which houses a collection of religious items and art.

The abbey is available to tourists and provides guided tours that emphasize its history and architectural aspects.

Additionally, the abbey is still an active site of worship and frequently hosts religious services, including mass and vespers.

In addition to its historical and architectural value, the Abbey of Saint-Victor de Marseille is also an important cultural and spiritual center for the city of Marseille. It has been a center of prayer and pilgrimage for centuries, and it continues to be a place where people gather to seek spiritual direction and inspiration.

The Abbey of Saint-Victor de Marseille is an important element of France's religious, cultural and architectural legacy. Visitors will be able to appreciate the ancient church and monastery and learn about its rich history and importance to the people of Marseille and the globe.

MuCEM

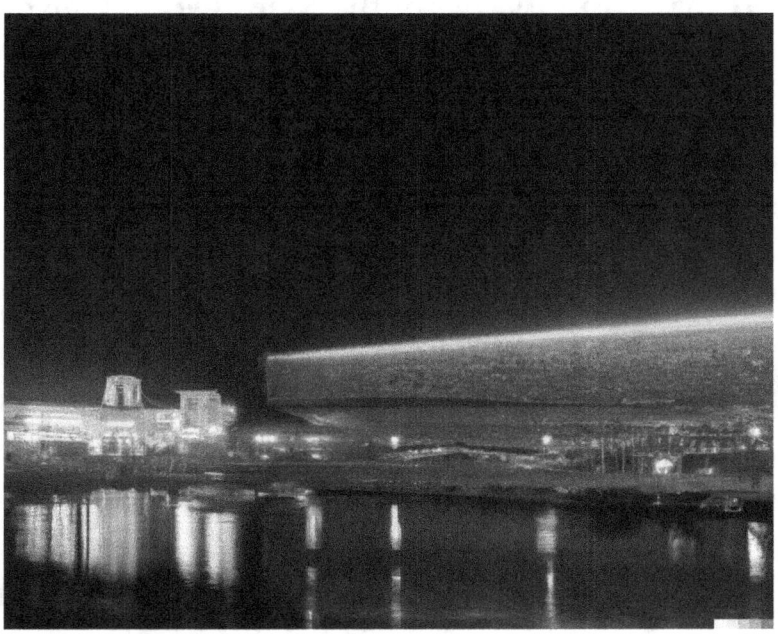

A view of the MuCEm at night

The MuCEM, or the Museum of European and Mediterranean Civilizations, is situated in Marseille, France and opened its doors to the public in 2013. The MuCEM is an architectural masterpiece, created by Rudy Ricciotti, that epitomizes the blending of the old and contemporary, highlighting the city's rich cultural legacy and its role in the Mediterranean world.

The museum is a tribute to the city's history and its importance in the Mediterranean area. It houses a wide collection of antiques, paintings, sculptures, and manuscripts, showing the cultural richness of the Mediterranean region and its peoples. The MuCEM's exhibitions extend from prehistory to the present day, illustrating the common cultural legacy of the Mediterranean area and the relationships that have produced its rich and varied civilizations.

One of the striking aspects of the MuCEM is its cutting-edge design. The museum's architecture fits perfectly with its surroundings, with the use of stone, wood, and glass to achieve a beautiful balance between the contemporary and the old.

The museum's main building is hung above the water, offering a spectacular view of the Old Port and the sea. The MuCEM also boasts a terrace that affords a stunning panoramic view of Marseille and the neighboring hills.

Visitors may explore the museum's numerous displays, including its permanent collection and rotating temporary exhibitions. The MuCEM also contains a research center, library, and a restaurant that offers traditional Mediterranean food. The museum's education section conducts courses and activities for children, teens, and adults, encouraging education and awareness of the different cultures of the Mediterranean area.

The MuCEM has swiftly become one of the most famous tourist sites in Marseille, receiving millions of tourists each year. It has garnered various prizes and plaudits for its unique architecture and its commitment to the development of the cultural heritage of the Mediterranean area.

The MuCEM is a must-visit place for anybody interested in history, culture, and architecture. With its unique combination of the ancient and the contemporary, it gives a fascinating view into the rich cultural legacy of the Mediterranean region and its varied civilizations. The museum is a tribute to the city of Marseille's role in the Mediterranean world and its dedication to conserving and promoting its cultural legacy for future generations to enjoy.

Petit Trianon

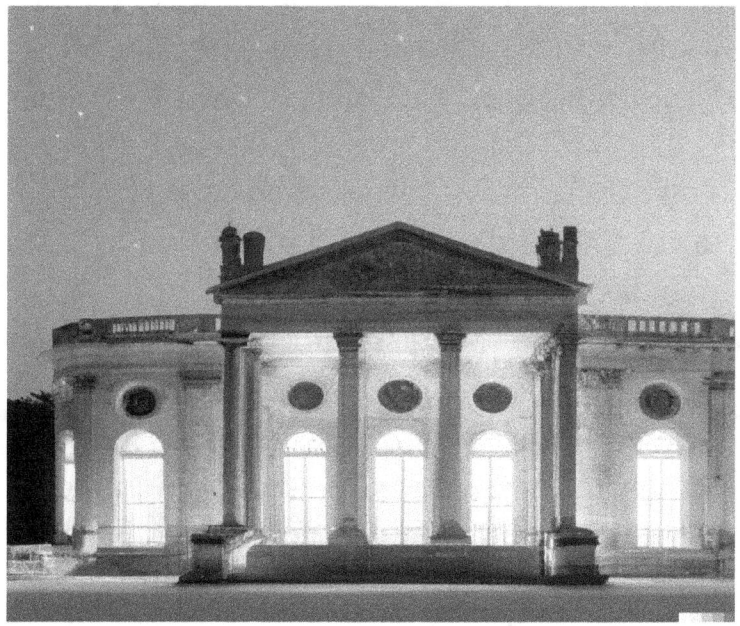

Petit Trianon

Petit Trianon is a modest palace situated in the Domain of Versailles in France. Built in the late 18th century, it was commissioned by King Louis XV as a private house for his lover, Madame de Pompadour. Later, it became the favorite hideaway of his successor, Queen Marie Antoinette. Today, Petit Trianon is a renowned tourist destination, recognized for its spectacular architecture, historical importance, and well-manicured gardens.

Petit Trianon was erected between 1762 and 1768, and was styled in the neoclassical style. The palace is tiny compared to the grandeur of Versailles, yet it is stylish and attractive in its own way. The structure comprises symmetrical wings and a center pavilion, surrounded by attractively planted grounds. The inside of the palace is as magnificent, with intricate moldings, gilt mirrors, and exquisite furniture.

Petit Trianon was initially planned as a private hideaway for King Louis XV and his lover, Madame de Pompadour. After Pompadour's death, the palace was frequented by various members of the French court, notably Marie Antoinette.

The queen fell in love with Petit Trianon and made it her personal refuge, utilizing it as a location to escape the formality of court life. She redecorated the palace in her own manner, and spent most of her time there, entertaining visitors and enjoying the grounds.

One of the most prominent characteristics of Petit Trianon is its gardens, which were planned by the famed French landscape architect, André Le Nôtre. The gardens are well kept, and contain geometric designs, fountains, and a diversity of flora and fauna. Visitors may wander around the paths, appreciating the grandeur of the gardens, or relax and have a picnic on the lawns.
Petit Trianon also has a great cultural and historical value. During the French Revolution, the palace was captured and served as a jail. After the Revolution, Petit Trianon was utilized for numerous

purposes, including a military hospital, a school, and a museum. Today, it is a museum and tourist attraction, drawing tourists from over the globe who are interested in the history of France and the French monarchy.

Petit Trianon is a magnificent chateau with a rich history, situated in the Domain of Versailles in France. It is noted for its neoclassical architecture, gorgeous gardens, and its link with King Louis XV and Queen Marie Antoinette. Whether you are interested in history, architecture, or gardening, Petit Trianon is a must-visit place in France.

Cathédrale Saint-André

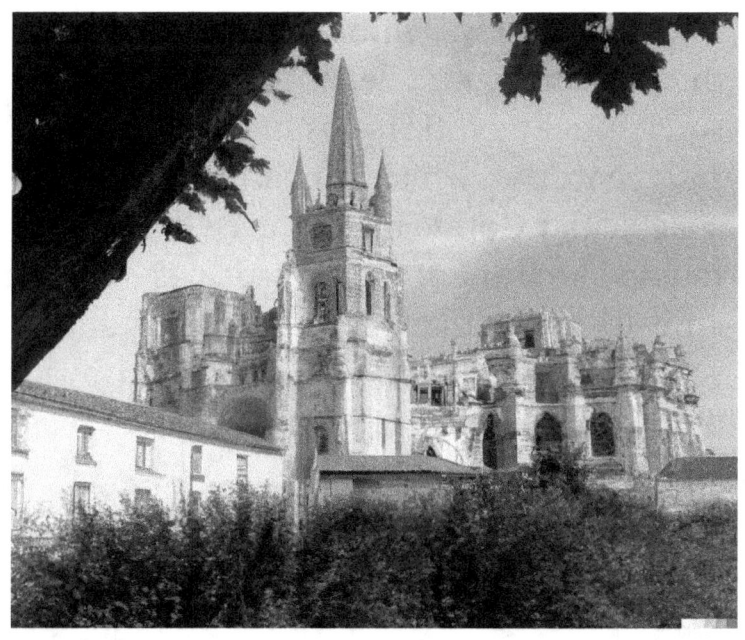
Cathédrale Saint-André

The Cathédrale Saint-André in Bordeaux, France, is a spectacular example of Gothic architecture and an essential part of the city's rich history. Dating back to the 12th century, this cathedral has been a center of devotion and pilgrimage for almost 900 years.

The cathedral was initially constructed in the Romanesque style, but received substantial modifications in the 13th and 14th centuries, which converted it into the spectacular Gothic masterpiece that it is today. The front of the cathedral is embellished with elaborate carvings and sculptures, featuring a beautiful portrayal of the Last Judgment above the great gateway.

Inside, the cathedral is just as spectacular, with towering arches and stained glass windows that reflect a warm, colorful light across the interior. The nave is lined with elaborate sculptures and carvings, and the high altar is flanked by a beautiful ensemble of stained glass windows.

One of the most prominent characteristics of the Cathédrale Saint-André is the collection of seven chapels, each devoted to a different saint. These chapels are embellished with exquisite paintings, sculptures, and stained glass windows, and serve as a tribute to the rich creative tradition of the area.

In addition to its religious significance, the Cathédrale Saint-André also retains a position of historical importance. During the French Revolution, the cathedral was utilized as a storage warehouse for wine, and afterwards as a location to store arms and ammunition. In the 19th century, the cathedral underwent substantial repairs to restore it to its former beauty, and today it is a famous tourist site and a revered emblem of Bordeaux's rich history and cultural legacy.

Whether you're a history enthusiast, an art lover, or just seeking for a tranquil spot to pause and reflect, the Cathédrale Saint-André is well worth a visit. With its breathtaking design, rich history, and lively cultural relevance, this cathedral is a tribute to the everlasting force of religion and the beauty of human creative expression. So, if you ever find yourself in Bordeaux, make sure to take a walk around the old streets and pay a visit to this wonderful cathedral.

The Cathédrale Saint-André is a stunning example of Gothic architecture and an essential component of Bordeaux's rich cultural history. With its exquisite carvings, spectacular stained glass windows, and rich history, this cathedral is a must-visit for anybody wishing to appreciate the rich creative and religious traditions of France.

Place de la Bourse

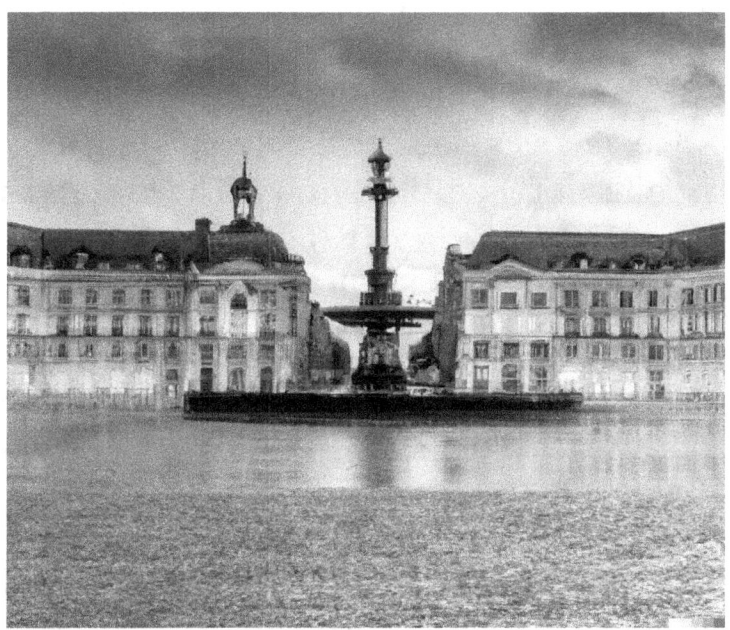

A view of Place de la Bourse

Place de la Bourse is a magnificent plaza situated in Bordeaux, France. This ancient area is surrounded by gorgeous 18th-century buildings and is recognized for its central fountain, which was erected in the late 1700s and has become a symbol of Bordeaux. The square is a major tourist site and draws tourists from all over the globe.

Place de la Bourse was created by Ange-Jacques Gabriel, a notable French architect of the 18th century. The plaza was established as part of a bigger initiative to restore the city of Bordeaux and to offer a central gathering area for its citizens. The square was finished in 1780 and rapidly became one of the most recognizable spots in the city.

The center fountain at Place de la Bourse is a wonderful piece of art and is one of the most photographed monuments in Bordeaux. The fountain is encircled by a wide basin that is filled with water, which reflects the gorgeous structures around the area. The fountain is also lighted up at night, which produces a spectacular spectacle that draws tourists from all around the city.

The structures around Place de la Bourse are remarkable masterpieces of art in their own right. They are famous examples of 18th-century French architecture and are noted for their complex features and graceful design. Many of the structures have been restored to their former condition and have become major tourist attractions. Visitors may take guided tours of the buildings to learn about their history and to view the spectacular architecture.

Place de la Bourse is also home to various museums, notably the Musée des Arts Décoratifs, which highlights French decorative arts from the 18th to the 20th century. The area is also home to the Musée d'Aquitaine, which gives an in-depth look at the history of Bordeaux and the surrounding region.

In addition to its historical and cultural features, Place de la Bourse is also a popular area for shopping and eating. The area is bordered by various cafés, restaurants, and stores that provide a broad variety of products and services. Visitors may have a meal or a drink while taking in the spectacular views of the plaza and its surroundings.

Place de la Bourse is a must-visit place for anybody visiting Bordeaux. This gorgeous area is a monument to the beauty and elegance of 18th-century French architecture and is surrounded by a plethora of cultural and historical treasures. Whether you're interested in history, art, or just enjoying a meal or a drink in a lovely environment, Spot de la Bourse is the right place to visit.

Colline de la Croix-Rousse

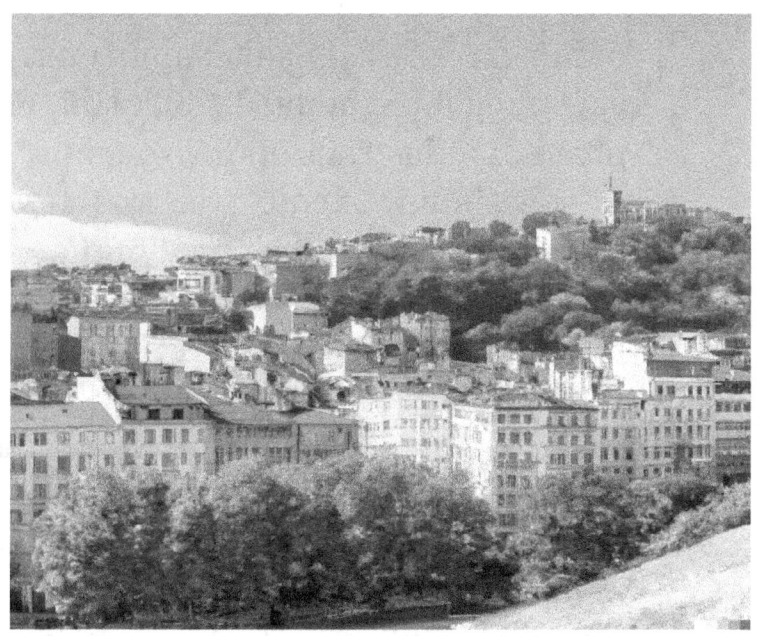

Colline de la Croix-Rousse

Colline de la Croix-Rousse, often known as La Colline, is a hill in the city of Lyon, France. It is noted for its cultural and historical importance, as well as its breathtaking views over the city.

The hill has a rich history, going back to the Roman Empire when it was utilized as a fortress. During the 19th century, it became a centre for silk manufacturing, garnering it the moniker "Silk Hill." This phase of industrialization brought a massive inflow of employees to the region, leading to the establishment of the dynamic neighborhood that still exists today.

One of the most prominent attractions of La Colline is its strong cultural environment. The hill is home to a variety of museums, theaters, and cultural institutes, including the Institut d'art Contemporain and the Maison des Canuts. The latter is a museum devoted to the history of silk manufacture in Lyon, giving a fascinating peek into the city's past.

Visitors to La Colline may also enjoy the numerous magnificent parks and gardens that dot the mountainside. Parc de la Tête d'Or is one of the most popular, giving a huge lake, picnic spaces, and lots of green space for people to rest in.

Another famous site in La Colline is Place des Terreaux, a big public area that acts as a gathering place for local people. The area is flanked by remarkable structures, including the Hôtel de Ville, the Musée des Beaux-Arts, and the Théâtre des Célestins.

In addition to its cultural activities, La Colline is also noted for its breathtaking views of the city. From the summit of the hill, tourists may take in panoramic views of Lyon and the surrounding landscape, including the Rhône River and the adjacent Monts du Lyonnais.

Despite its appeal as a tourist attraction, La Colline has also been acknowledged for its attempts to protect its cultural legacy.

The area is home to a variety of conserved buildings and historical landmarks, including the typical traboules (small passageways) that were previously utilized by silk producers to convey their wares.

Colline de la Croix-Rousse is a unique and intriguing area in the city of Lyon, France. With its rich history, thriving cultural life, and magnificent vistas, it is a must-visit place for anybody visiting the area. Whether you're a history buff, an art enthusiast, or just seeking a vacation from the city, La Colline has something to offer everyone.

Fountains of Versailles

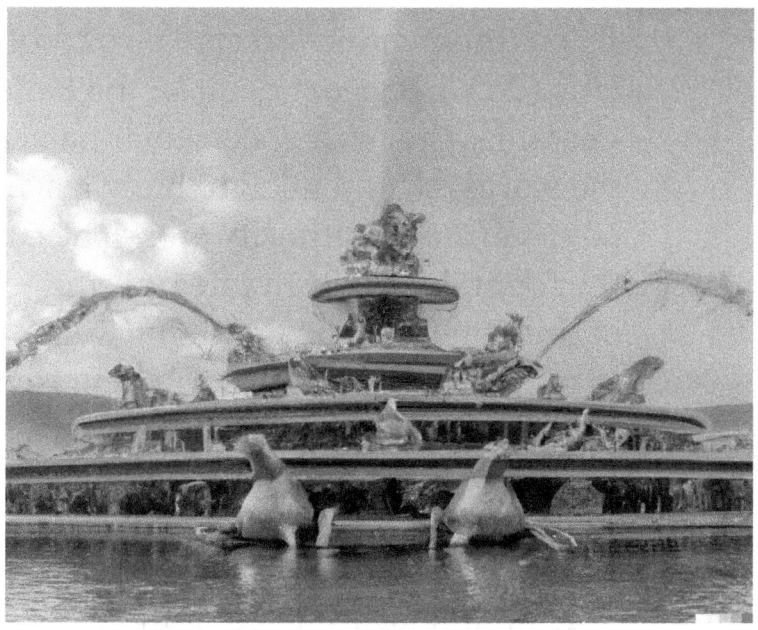

A view of the Fountain of Versailles

The Fountains of Versailles in France are among the most majestic and breathtaking architectural wonders in the world. They were erected in the 17th century during the reign of King Louis XIV and are regarded to be one of the finest masterpieces of French Baroque architecture.

The fountains were erected as part of King Louis XIV's big goal to make the Palace of Versailles the most spectacular palace in the world. He intended to build a symbol of his ultimate authority and riches, and the fountains were an integral component of this concept. The fountains were created to reflect the king's authority and riches, and their beauty and grandeur have made a lasting effect on visitors to the palace for centuries.

The fountains at Versailles are known for their elaborate and exquisite design, and they are regarded to be among the best specimens of Baroque architecture in the world. The fountains are placed amid the palace's wide and picturesque gardens, which are ornamented with a variety of lovely flowers, shrubs, and trees.

The major highlight of the fountains is the Grand Trianon, which is a large fountain that sits in the middle of the garden. It is flanked by smaller fountains and sculptures, producing a beautiful and harmonious display of water and light. Another notable fountain at Versailles is the Latona Fountain, which was created to honor the fable of the goddess Latona and her children, who were transformed into frogs.

The fountains are not only attractive but also practical. They were built to provide the palace with water and to act as a source of pleasure and amusement for the court. During the summer months, musical events were conducted in the gardens, and the fountains were switched on to give a spectacular show of light and water. The fountains were also employed to cool the castle during hot summer days.

Today, the Fountains of Versailles are a renowned tourist site, drawing millions of people each year. The fountains are still in service, and they are often switched on to present tourists with a spectacular show of water and light. Visitors may take guided tours of the palace and grounds, and they can also enjoy a range of other attractions, such as the famed Hall of Mirrors, which was used as a ballroom by the French royal court.

The Fountains of Versailles are a tribute to the grandeur and extravagance of the French Baroque period. They are among the most stunning architectural wonders in the world, and they continue to attract tourists with their beauty and majesty. The fountains are a must-see for anybody who is interested in French history and architecture, and they are a symbol of King Louis XIV's goal to make the Palace of

Versailles the most spectacular palace in the world.

Musee D'Orsay

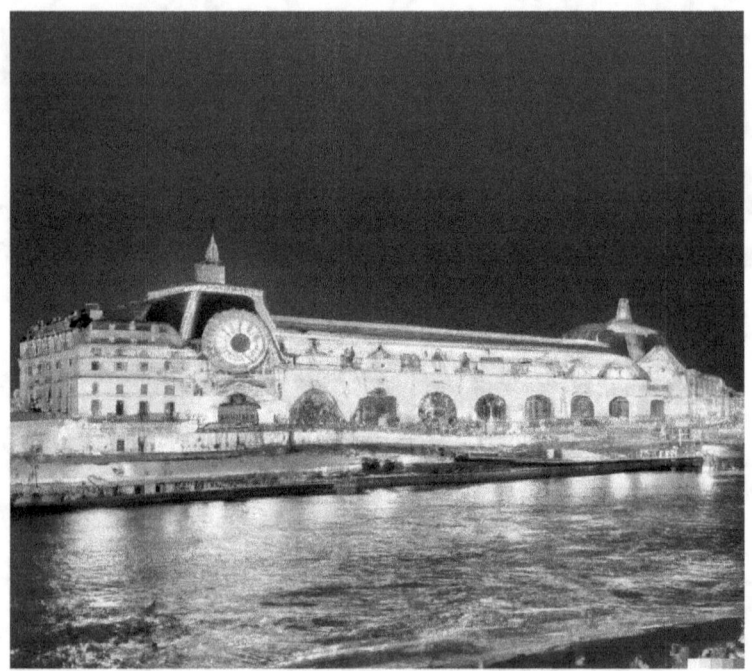

Musee d'Orsay

Musee d'Orsay is a museum situated in Paris, France, built in a former railway station on the left side of the Seine. It is one of the greatest art museums in Europe and is recognized for its huge collection of

Impressionist and Post-Impressionist masterpieces. The museum is named after the Gare d'Orsay, the station it was located in, which was established in 1900 and used as a train station until 1939.

The museum's collection includes works by some of the most famous artists of the 19th and early 20th centuries, such as Edgar Degas, Pierre-Auguste Renoir, Claude Monet, Berthe Morisot, Mary Cassatt, Gustave Caillebotte, Gustave Courbet, Édouard Manet, Berthe Morisot, Edgar Degas, and Henri Toulouse-Lautrec. Visitors may enjoy a huge number of paintings, sculptures, and decorative arts, including furniture and pottery, as well as a big number of drawings, photos, and other works on paper.

In addition to the Impressionist collection, the Musee d'Orsay also shows works from other key art styles of the 19th and early

20th century, including Romanticism, Realism, and Symbolism. Visitors may examine works by notable painters such as Eugène Delacroix, Jean-Auguste-Dominique Ingres, and Théodore Géricault, as well as specimens of Art Nouveau and Art Deco styles.

The museum's remarkable architecture and attractive location further contribute to its attraction. The building itself is a piece of beauty, with its distinctive façade and lofty, arched windows that allow enough natural light. Inside, the vast galleries are adorned with beautifully crafted ornamental moldings and marble flooring, giving a breathtaking background for the art on show.

In addition to its permanent collection, the Musee d'Orsay also periodically presents special exhibits, which might concentrate on a specific artist, movement, or topic.

These exhibits enable visitors to examine pieces from other collections, both from France and beyond, and give a unique chance to obtain a better knowledge of the art on show.

Visitors to the Musee d'Orsay may also take advantage of the museum's educational programs and guided tours, which are provided in numerous languages. These events allow visitors the opportunity to learn more about the pieces on show and the artists who produced them, and may provide a deeper understanding of the art.

In conclusion, the Musee d'Orsay is a must-visit site for anybody who loves art and is interested in the works of the Impressionist and Post-Impressionist movements. With its enormous collection, gorgeous location, and frequent special exhibits, the museum provides something for everyone and is guaranteed to create a memorable experience.

Sainte-Chapelle

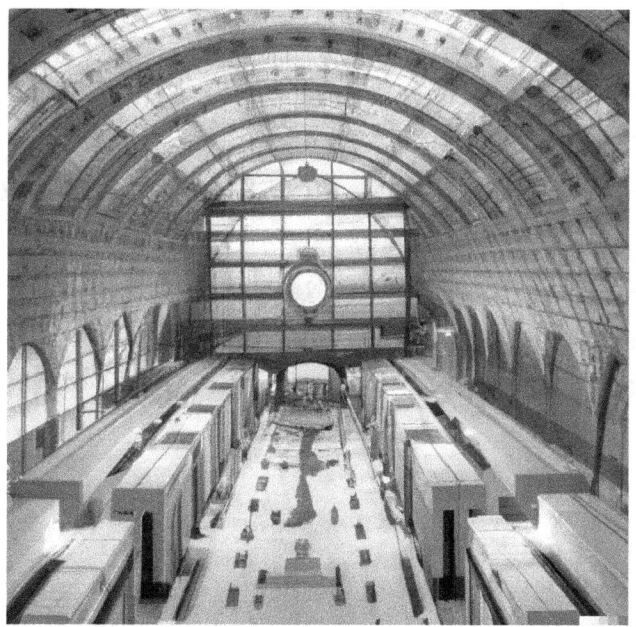

Sainte-Chapelle interior view.

Sainte-Chapelle is a strikingly beautiful and ancient medieval chapel situated in the center of Paris, France. This stunning architectural marvel was erected in the mid-13th century and is usually regarded as one of the most significant examples of Gothic architecture in the world.

The Sainte-Chapelle was initially commissioned by King Louis IX to contain a collection of Christian relics, including the Crown of Thorns, that he had obtained during a visit to the Holy Land. The chapel was created as an addition to the royal residence on the Ile de la Cité, and its construction was finished in under 7 years.

One of the distinctive characteristics of Sainte-Chapelle is its spectacular stained glass windows, which span over three-quarters of the chapel's walls and rise up to 50 feet into the air. The brilliant colors and detailed patterns of the glass reflect scenes from the Old and New Testaments of the Bible, as well as tales from the lives of the saints. The windows are not only attractive but also serve as an educational aid for individuals who may not have been able to read or comprehend the printed word.

In addition to its spectacular stained glass, the Sainte-Chapelle is also noted for its graceful and delicate architecture, with its thin columns and ribbed vaults generating a sensation of lightness and airiness. The chapel's two levels also exhibit the distinct forms of Gothic architecture, with the lower level displaying the early Gothic style, while the top level represents the more elaborate Rayonnant style.

Despite its fragile look, Sainte-Chapelle has proved to be a very strong architecture, weathering centuries of political and religious change, as well as several wars and natural calamities. During the French Revolution, the chapel was almost destroyed, but was preserved by the efforts of a group of art enthusiasts who encouraged the government to save it.

Today, Sainte-Chapelle continues to be a renowned tourist site, drawing tourists from all over the globe who come to appreciate its spectacular beauty and rich history. In addition to its usual visiting hours, the chapel also offers special events and performances throughout the year, enabling visitors to experience its splendor in a new and memorable manner.

Sainte-Chapelle is a superb example of medieval architecture and one of the most beautiful and historically important chapels in the world. It's gorgeous stained glass windows, delicate construction, and rich history make it a must-visit for anybody visiting Paris, and a genuine tribute to the lasting splendor of medieval art and architecture.

Montmartre

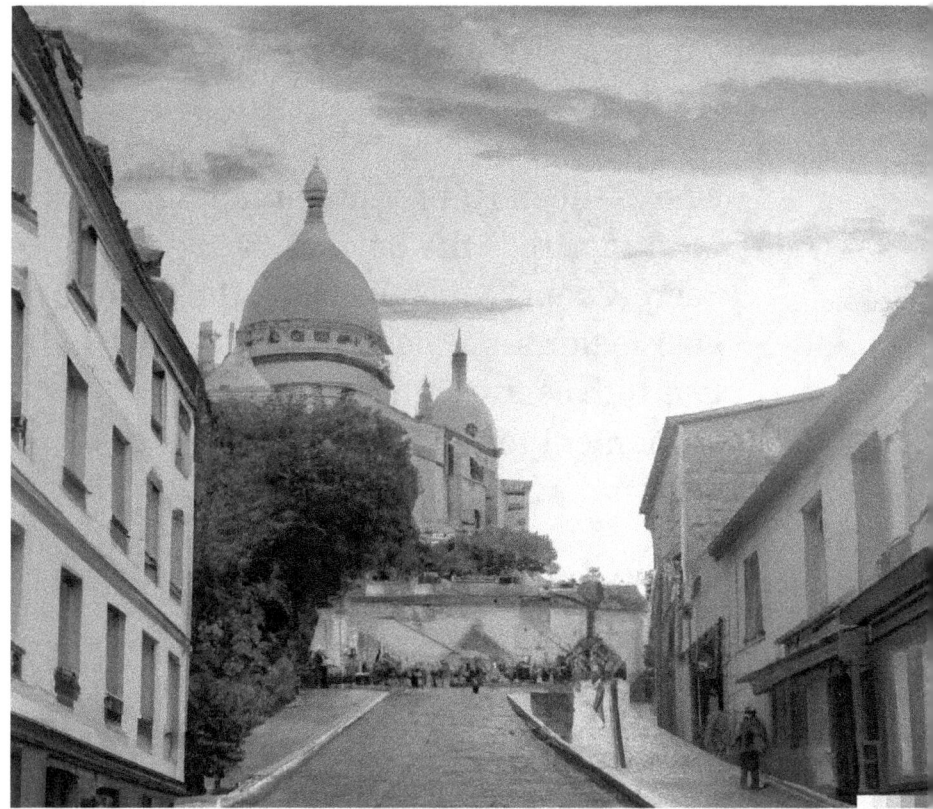

Montmartre

Montmartre is a historic hilltop suburb situated in the 18th arrondissement of

Paris, France. Known for its breathtaking views of the city, picturesque streets, and bohemian vibe, Montmartre has long been a popular destination for visitors and residents alike.

One of the most prominent monuments in Montmartre is the Basilica of the Sacré-Coeur, which lies atop the hill and gives panoramic views of Paris. Built in the late 19th century, the basilica is a monument to the area's history as a destination of prayer and pilgrimage.

Another famous destination in Montmartre is the Place du Tertre, a picturesque plaza surrounded by cafés and artists selling their works. This area was originally a favorite meeting spot for artists such as Pablo Picasso, Amedeo Modigliani, and Vincent van Gogh, and it remains a dynamic center of creativity to this day.

In addition to its cultural past, Montmartre is also recognized for its bustling nightlife. The district is home to several pubs, clubs, and cabarets, including the famed Moulin Rouge. Here, tourists may experience a genuine French cabaret presentation, replete with feathers, glitter, and champagne.

One of the finest ways to see Montmartre is on foot, since the tiny lanes and steep slopes make it unsuitable for automobiles. As you explore around the area, you'll uncover secret squares, beautiful cafés, and gorgeous passageways. Be sure to stop by the Place des Abbesses, a picturesque plaza dotted by cafés and street performers, and the Place Dalida, a modest square devoted to the great French singer.

For those interested in history, a visit to the Montmartre Museum is a must. This museum is based in the old studio of

French painter Gustave Moreau and highlights the neighborhood's rich creative legacy via a collection of paintings, sketches, and sculptures.

Montmartre is a distinctive and lovely area that gives an insight into Paris's rich history and creative legacy. Whether you're wanting to enjoy beautiful vistas, experience the city's dynamic nightlife, or just take in the sights and sounds of a historic neighborhood, Montmartre is a must-visit place for anybody visiting Paris.

Musee Rodin

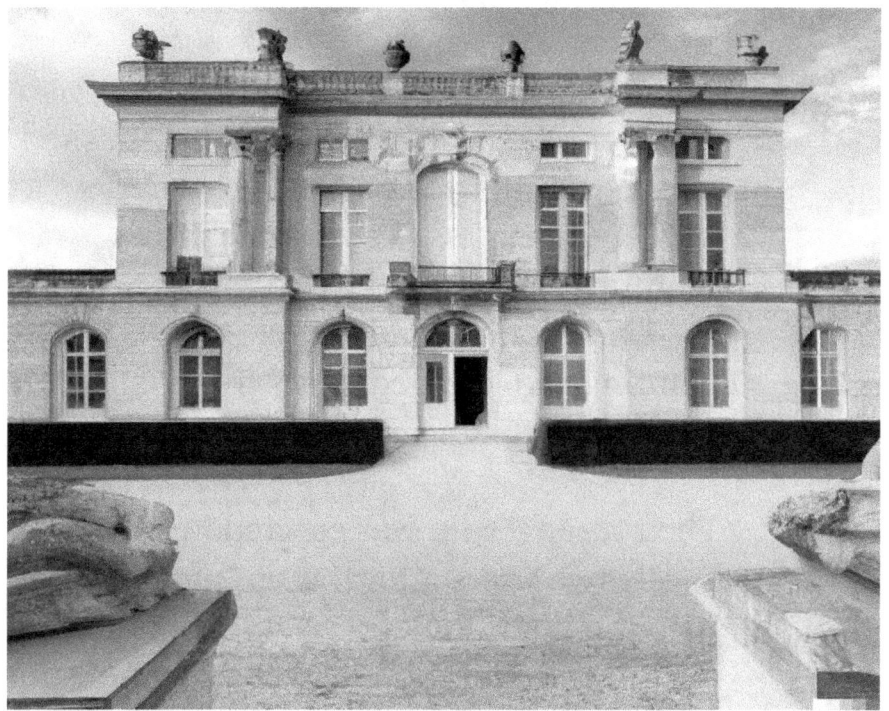

Musee Rodin

The Musée Rodin in Paris, France, is a museum devoted to the works of the famed French artist, Auguste Rodin. Located in the center of Paris, this museum is built in an 18th-century townhouse and includes a significant collection of Rodin's sculptures, sketches, and personal things.

Auguste Rodin was a revolutionary sculptor who broke away from established methods of the period and pioneered a new, more expressive approach to sculpting. He is well known for works such as "The Thinker" and "The Kiss". His paintings are defined by their realism, passion, and movement.

The Musée Rodin was created in 1919, barely two years after the sculptor's death, with the intention of conserving his works for future generations. Today, the museum is home to nearly 6,000 sculptures, sketches, and artefacts relating to Rodin. Visitors may explore the museum's permanent collection, which includes some of the sculptor's most renowned works, as well as temporary exhibits that emphasize certain elements of his life and work.

One of the centerpieces of the Musée Rodin is the Garden of Rodin. This stunning outdoor setting is home to some of the sculptor's most renowned works, including "The Thinker", "The Burghers of Calais", and "The Gates of Hell". The garden is also a calm refuge in the center of the city, and visitors may rest on the lawns or sit on the benches while viewing the sculptures.

In addition to the permanent collection and temporary exhibits, the Musée Rodin also provides a range of educational activities for visitors of all ages. Guided tours, seminars, and family activities are just a few of the alternatives offered, making this museum a great location for families, students, and art enthusiasts of all ages.

The Musée Rodin is also a fantastic spot for art enthusiasts to acquire unusual and creative presents. The museum's store provides a broad selection of merchandise inspired by Rodin's work, including books, replicas of his sculptures, and jewelry.

The Musée Rodin is a must-visit location for everyone who is interested in art, sculpture, or French culture. With its enormous collection of Rodin's sculptures and lovely garden, this museum provides a memorable experience for visitors of all ages. Whether you are an art fan or just searching for a tranquil respite in the center of the city, the Musée Rodin is a wonderful location.

Luxembourg Palace

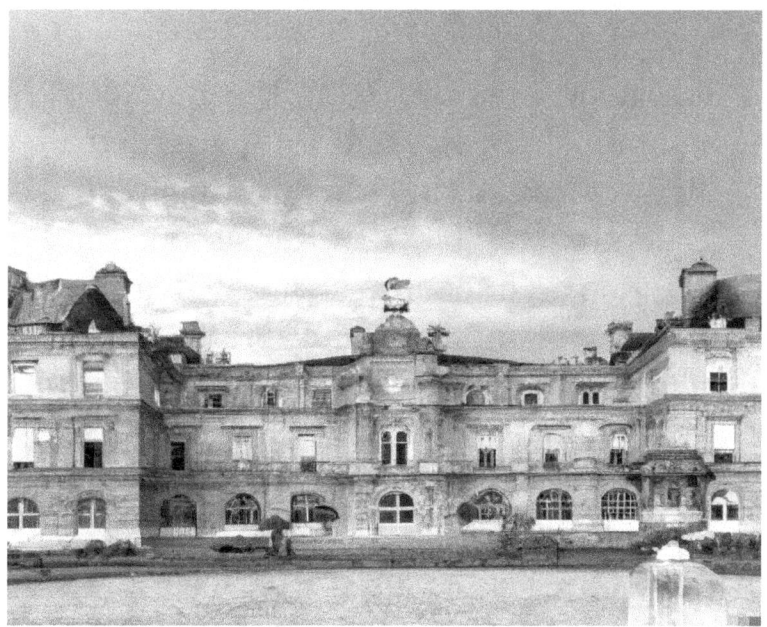

The Luxembourg Palace

The Luxembourg Palace, situated in the centre of Paris, France, is a historic edifice with a rich history and cultural value. Originally erected in the early 17th century as a house for Marie de' Medici, the mother of King Louis XIII, the palace has served different roles over the ages, including acting as the site of the French Senate.

The palace was created by the architect Salomon de Brosse and was patterned after the Palazzo Pitti in Florence, Italy. The structure has a blend of Renaissance and Baroque architectural styles, with a central courtyard flanked by multiple wings. The inside of the palace is just as stunning, with its opulent chambers, massive staircases, and exquisite pieces of art.

One of the features of the palace is the Luxembourg Garden, a lovely public garden that comprises over 25 acres of ground. The area is home to various antiquities, including the Medici Fountain, which was completed in 1630. The park also boasts a variety of gardens, including the French Garden, the English Garden, and the Garden of the Queen.

The Luxembourg Palace has had a long and diverse history, acting as a jail during the French Revolution and as a museum under Napoleon Bonaparte. It was subsequently utilized as a hospital during World War I and as a cultural center during World War II.

In the late 19th and early 20th centuries, the palace was refurbished and restored to its former splendor. Today, the Luxembourg Palace is a major tourist destination, drawing tourists from over the globe who come to appreciate its architectural beauty and historical value.

The palace is also home to the French Senate, making it a symbol of the country's political strength. The Senate meets in the palace's great rooms, where it performs its business and considers major problems confronting the nation.

Visitors to the Luxembourg Palace may take a guided tour of the palace, which gives a rare chance to understand its rich history and cultural importance. The trip provides access to some of the palace's most renowned rooms, including the grand staircase, the salon of the Hercules, and the salon of the Abundance.

The Luxembourg Palace is a must-visit location for anybody interested in French history and culture. Its rich history, spectacular architecture, and breathtaking surroundings make it a really unique and fascinating location to visit. Whether you're a history buff, an architectural admirer, or just someone searching for a lovely park in the middle of Paris, the Luxembourg Palace is the right location.

Place De La Concorde

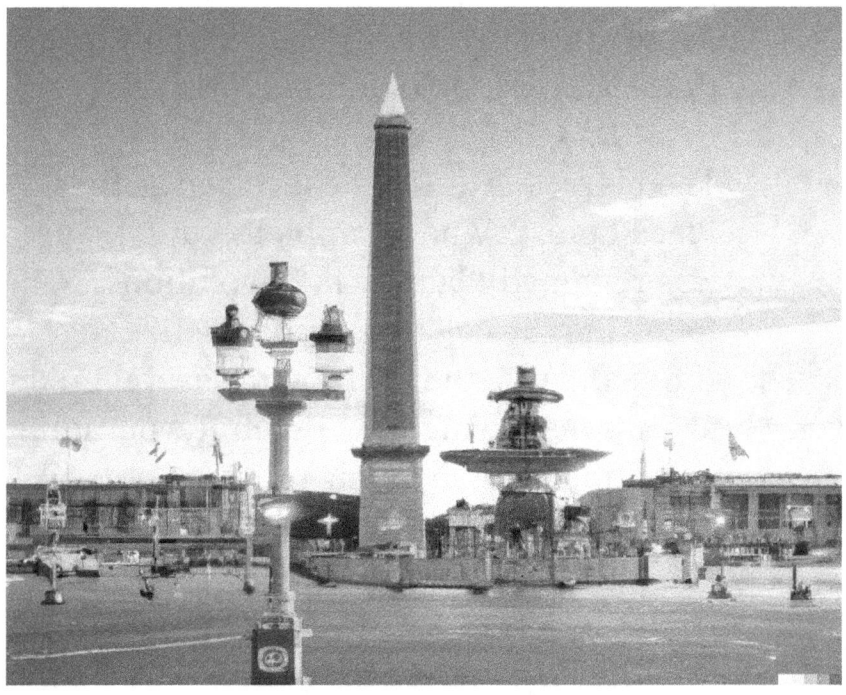

Place de la Concorde

Place de la Concorde is one of the most renowned and historic public squares in France, situated in the center of Paris between the Tuileries Gardens and the

Champs-Elysées. It has a rich and dramatic past, having served as the scene of various significant periods in French history, notably the French Revolution and the reign of Napoleon Bonaparte.

The plaza was initially conceived as the Place Louis XV and completed in 1755. It was renamed Place de la Revolution following the collapse of the Bastille in 1789, and was the location of several public executions during the French Revolution, including the beheading of King Louis XVI in 1793.

In the 19th century, the area was renovated into the Place de la Concorde, created by architect Jacques-Ange Gabriel. The area was ornamented with the famed Fontaine des Mers and the Fontaine des Fleuves, which represent the oceans and rivers of France. In the heart of the plaza sits the majestic Obelisk of Luxor, a gift from the viceroy of Egypt to King Louis-Philippe in 1836.

During the reign of Napoleon Bonaparte, the plaza was utilized as a military parade field, and it was afterwards the venue of numerous notable political rallies and marches. Today, the Place de la Concorde is a major tourist destination, bringing tourists from over the globe to see its stunning fountains, majestic architecture, and iconic obelisk.

One of the most renowned structures on the plaza is the Hôtel de Crillon, a magnificent hotel that has entertained many historic visitors, including Marie Antoinette and Louis XVI. The Hôtel de la Marine, situated on the western side of the plaza, was the headquarters of the French Navy during the era of Napoleon, and now it houses the French Naval Ministry.

The Place de la Concorde is also home to numerous major monuments and memorials, notably the Memorial des Martyrs de la Deportation, dedicated to the victims of the Nazi deportations during World War II. The area also serves as a popular meeting place for Parisians and foreigners alike, holding events like the annual Fête Nationale and performances by the Orchestre de Paris.

Despite its history of bloodshed and political instability, Place de la Concorde remains one of the most beautiful and famous public venues in France. With its spectacular architecture, fountains, and monuments, it continues to draw people from across the globe who come to appreciate its beauty and rich history. Whether you are a history buff or just a fan of gorgeous public spaces, Place de la Concorde is a must-see site for anybody visiting Paris.

Place de la Concorde is a crucial element of French history and culture, having served as the venue of countless major political and social events over the years.
Today, it is a popular tourist site and meeting place for Parisians and visitors alike, giving a spectacular example of French architecture and design, and a tribute to the rich and diverse history of France.

Musée de l'Orangerie

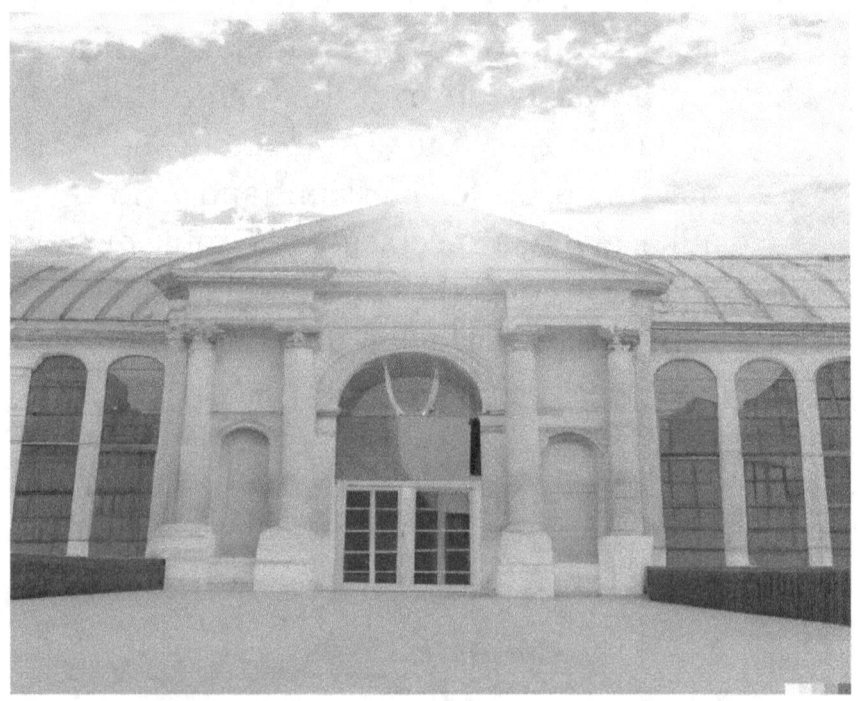

Musée de l'Orangerie

Musée de l'Orangerie is a museum in Paris, France that is famous for its collection of Impressionist and Post-Impressionist paintings. The museum is located in the

Tuileries Garden and was originally built as a greenhouse for orange trees in the late 19th century. Today, it is one of the most important museums in France, attracting thousands of visitors every year.

The museum is best known for its eight large oval paintings by the French Impressionist Claude Monet. These paintings, known as the Water Lilies, are considered some of Monet's greatest works and depict the artist's flower garden at Giverny. The Water Lilies are displayed in two oval rooms that were specially designed to showcase the paintings, creating a unique and immersive experience for visitors.

In addition to the Water Lilies, the museum also has an extensive collection of works by other famous Impressionists and Post-Impressionists, including Pierre-Auguste Renoir, Henri Matisse, and

Pablo Picasso. These works are displayed in several galleries throughout the museum, offering a comprehensive overview of the development of modern art in France.

One of the highlights of the museum is its collection of Renoir's Nudes, which are considered some of the artist's most beautiful and sensual works. The Nudes are displayed in a series of interconnected galleries that are designed to highlight the artist's use of light and color. Another notable feature of the museum is its collection of works by Henri Matisse, including his famous Jazz series, which are considered some of his most important works.

In addition to its collection of paintings, Musée de l'Orangerie also has a library and archives that are open to researchers and art historians. The library contains a wealth of resources on the history of Impressionism and Post-Impressionism, including books, journals, and manuscripts. The archives contain a wealth of information on the museum's collection, including photographs, letters, and documents related to the artists and their works.

Visitors to Musée de l'Orangerie are also able to take advantage of the museum's educational programs, including guided tours, workshops, and lectures. These programs provide visitors with an in-depth understanding of the museum's collection and the artists who created the works.

Musée de l'Orangerie is a must-visit for anyone interested in modern art and the history of Impressionism and Post-Impressionism. With its exceptional collection of works by Monet, Renoir, Matisse, and other famous artists, the museum offers a unique and immersive experience for visitors. Whether you're a seasoned art lover or just curious about the history of modern art, Musée de l'Orangerie is a truly remarkable museum that is not to be missed.

Pere Lachaise Cemetery

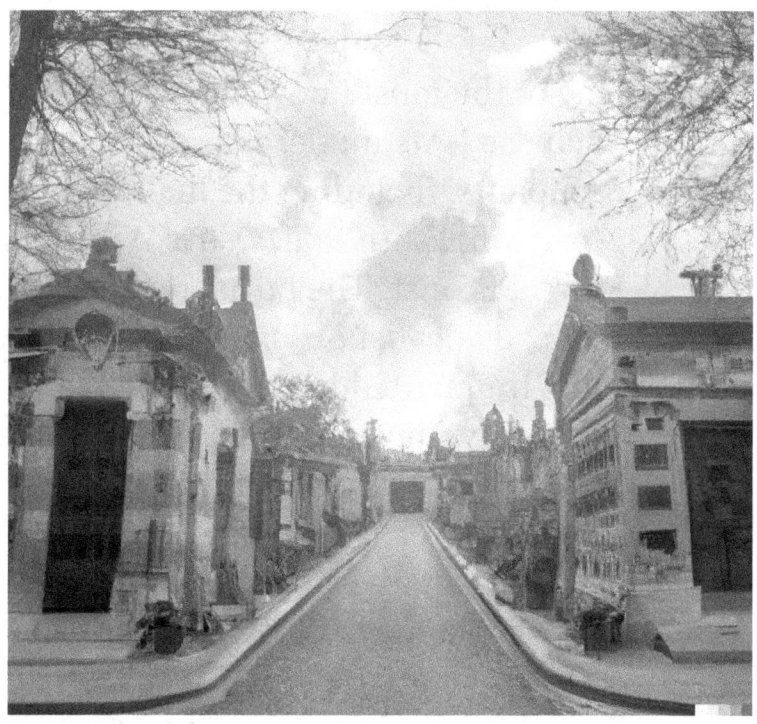

Père Lachaise Cemetery

Père Lachaise Cemetery is one of the most renowned cemeteries in the world, situated in Paris, France. Founded in 1804, it is the biggest cemetery in the city and houses the graves of some of the most prominent and well-known personalities in French and international history.

One of the most known elements of Père Lachaise is its numerous renowned occupants, including the likes of Jim Morrison, Edith Piaf, Oscar Wilde, and Marcel Proust. The burial of Jim Morrison, the lead vocalist of The Doors, is one of the most frequented in the cemetery and has become a pilgrimage place for followers from across the globe. Edith Piaf, the great French singer, is also buried in the cemetery and her tomb draws innumerable fans who come to pay their respects.

The cemetery is also home to a variety of magnificent sculptures, notably the exquisite monuments that decorate the graves of many of the most notable persons buried there. Some of the most stunning pieces of art are the statue of

Oscar Wilde, which represents him resting on a stone bench in repose, and the marble angel that marks the tomb of Marcel Proust, which is regarded one of the most beautiful in the cemetery.

One of the remarkable qualities of Père Lachaise is its size and arrangement. The cemetery comprises over 110 acres and is filled with meandering walks, rich foliage, and quiet ponds, providing a pleasant and serene ambiance that is in sharp contrast to the busy metropolis beyond its gates. Despite its immensity, the cemetery is well-organized and visitors may easily make their way around using the thorough map and guidebook given at the entry.

Père Lachaise Cemetery is not merely a place of rest for the dead, but it is also a site of inspiration for the living. The tranquil settings, stunning sculptures, and historical importance of the cemetery have made it a favorite place for authors, painters, and photographers, who come to capture its particular beauty and feeling of timelessness. It is also a major tourist site, drawing millions of tourists each year who come to pay their respects to the great personalities buried there and to enjoy its rich history and cultural legacy.

Père Lachaise Cemetery is a unique and intriguing area that mixes the tranquility of a serene park with the rich history and cultural legacy of one of the world's most significant cities. Whether you are a history enthusiast, a follower of the arts, or just searching for a calm getaway from the rush and bustle of daily life, Père Lachaise is well worth a visit.

Palais Garnier Opera House

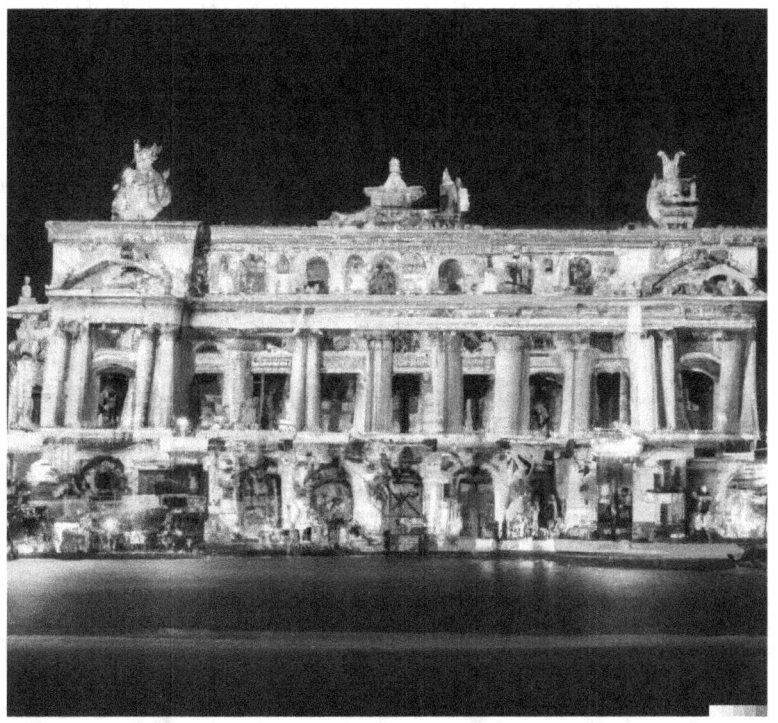

Palais Garnier at night

Palais Garnier is one of the most prominent opera theaters in the world.

Located in the center of Paris, France, this spectacular structure was created by architect Charles Garnier and opened its doors to the public in 1875. Since then, it has been a cultural and architectural symbol in the city, drawing millions of people each year.

The Palais Garnier is a masterpiece of Second Empire architecture and is regarded as one of the greatest examples of the Beaux-Arts style. Its architecture incorporates a blend of classical and contemporary elements, with a vast, imposing exterior and a grand staircase leading to the entry hall. The building's inside is just as magnificent, with intricate embellishments, gilded moldings, and marble statues.

One of the most outstanding aspects of the Palais Garnier is its large, central chandelier that hangs from the roof of the great theater. The chandelier weighs more than 6 tons and features 6,000 lights, making it one of the biggest in the world. The theatre is furnished with rich, red velvet seats and soft, gold-embroidered drapes, giving it a beautiful backdrop for performances.

The Palais Garnier has been the home of the Paris Opera since its inauguration and has held many of the world's most renowned operas and ballets throughout the years. From Tchaikovsky's "Swan Lake" to Puccini's "Tosca," the Palais Garnier has witnessed innumerable productions and performances, solidifying its reputation as one of the world's great opera theaters.

In addition to its artistic value, the Palais Garnier is also a significant historical site. It was utilized as a backdrop for the 1910 book "The Phantom of the Opera" by

Gaston Leroux and has since been the basis for various versions of the narrative, including a long-running musical and multiple films. Today, visitors to the Palais Garnier may enjoy guided tours of the building and learn about its rich history and cultural legacy.

The Palais Garnier continues to serve a significant role in the cultural life of Paris, holding performances of opera, ballet, and classical music for audiences from across the globe. Whether you're a devotee of the arts or just admire gorgeous architecture, a visit to the Palais Garnier is a must for everyone visiting Paris. So, if you are planning a vacation to the City of Light, make sure to take in the grandeur and elegance of this great opera theater.

The Palais Garnier is a spectacular example of Second Empire architecture and a cultural icon in Paris. Its rich history, breathtaking architecture, and world-renowned performances make it a must-visit location for anybody interested in the arts or the history of Paris.

Boulevards Legendary Cafés

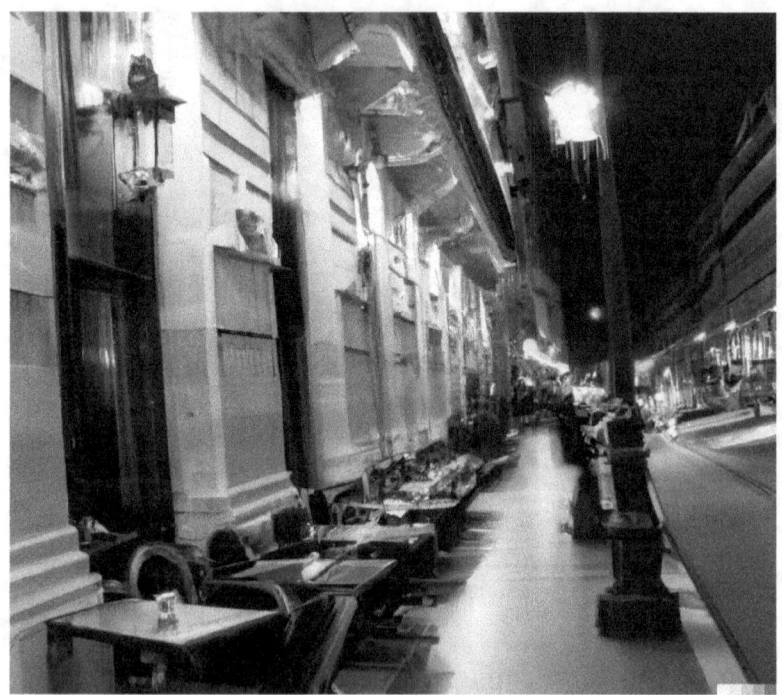

Boulevards Legendary Cafés

France is famous for its rich culture, stunning architecture, and world-renowned cuisine. From the historic avenues of Paris to the charming streets of the countryside, there's a lot to explore in the country. One of the best ways to experience the true essence of France is to take a walk down its bustling boulevards and visit its legendary cafes.

Boulevards in France are a hub of activity and are lined with shops, cafes, and restaurants. The most famous boulevard in France is the Champs-Élysées in Paris, which is considered the most beautiful avenue in the world. This iconic street is home to many luxury stores, theaters, cinemas, and cafes, making it one of the most popular tourist destinations in the country. Another famous boulevard in

France is the Boulevard Saint-Germain, located in the heart of Paris. This street is famous for its cultural and artistic heritage, and it's home to many famous cafes such as Les Deux Magots and Café de

Flore, both of which have been frequented by many famous artists, writers, and intellectuals over the years.

Cafes in France are an integral part of the country's culture and are considered a meeting place for friends and family. From early morning coffee and croissants to evening drinks and light bites, cafes offer a place for people to relax, socialize, and enjoy the company of others.

One of the most famous cafes in France is Café de la Paix, located in the heart of Paris. This historic cafe, established in 1862, is known for its beautiful decor and offers a stunning view of the Opéra Garnier. Another famous cafe in France is Le Café des Arts, located in the picturesque town of Avignon. This cafe is famous for its delicious coffee, warm atmosphere, and live music, making it a popular spot for locals and tourists alike.

France's bustling boulevards and legendary cafes are an important part of the country's rich cultural heritage. These iconic places offer a unique experience to visitors and provide a glimpse into the true essence of France. Whether you're in Paris, Avignon, or any other city in France, taking a walk down its boulevards and stopping at its cafes is a must-do for anyone looking to truly experience the country's culture and history.

Place Massena

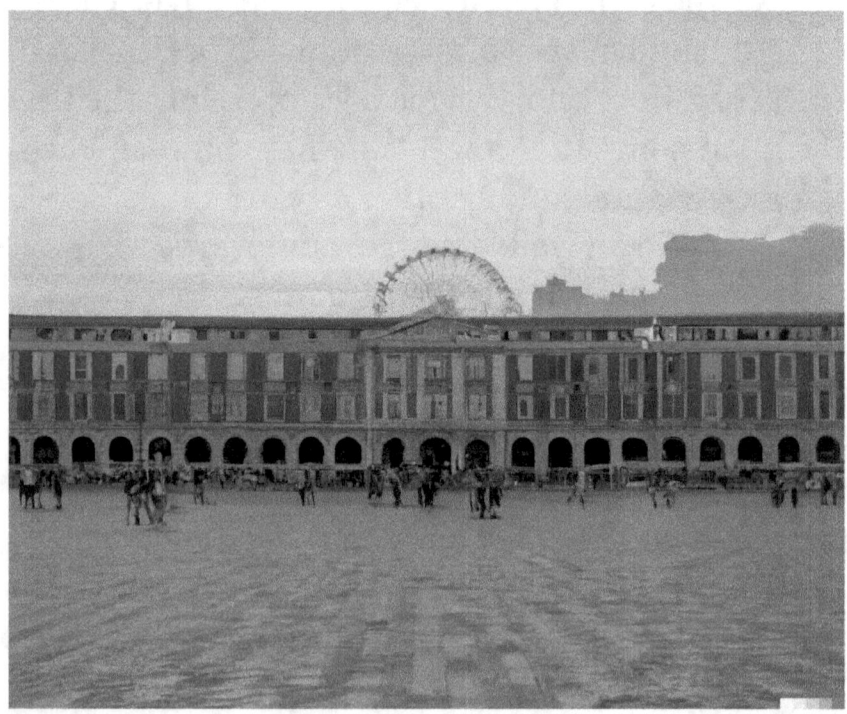

Place Massena

Place Massena is a bustling plaza situated in the centre of Nice, France. It is one of the city's key sights and draws millions of tourists every year. The area is surrounded by majestic architecture, lovely fountains, and stunning gardens, making it a great spot for travelers to rest and take in the sights and sounds of the city.

The area was named for André Masséna, a great French general who played a crucial part in Napoleon's army. The neighborhood was initially created in the 19th century and has subsequently undergone various restorations to enhance its aesthetic and functioning. Today, Area Massena is a popular meeting place for residents and visitors alike and is regularly the scene of festivals, concerts, and other events.

One of the greatest attractions of Place Massena is its stunning fountains. The area is home to two gigantic fountains that are lighted at night, providing a beautiful show of light and water. The fountains are surrounded by thick vegetation and beautiful gardens, giving tourists a calm refuge in the center of the city.

Another aspect of Place Massena is its architecture. The area is flanked by exquisite structures, many of which date back to the 19th century. Some of the more prominent structures are the Palais de la Prefecture, the Hotel Regina, and the Hotel Negresco. These old monuments are a tribute to the city's rich architectural past and offer a wonderful background for tourists to explore.

In addition to its beauty, Place Massena is also a hive of activity. The area is dotted with stores, cafés, and restaurants, making it the ideal spot for people to gather together and enjoy the city's rich culture. From small shops to high-end brand retailers, there's something for everyone at Place Massena. The area is also home to numerous renowned cafés and restaurants, providing tourists a fantastic array of food and drink choices.

Here is a must-visit for anybody experiencing the city. Whether you're a native or a visitor, you'll find something to appreciate about this magnificent plaza. From its gorgeous fountains to its exquisite architecture and bustling ambiance, Place Massena is certainly a treasure of the French Riviera.

St Nicholas Orthodox Cathedral

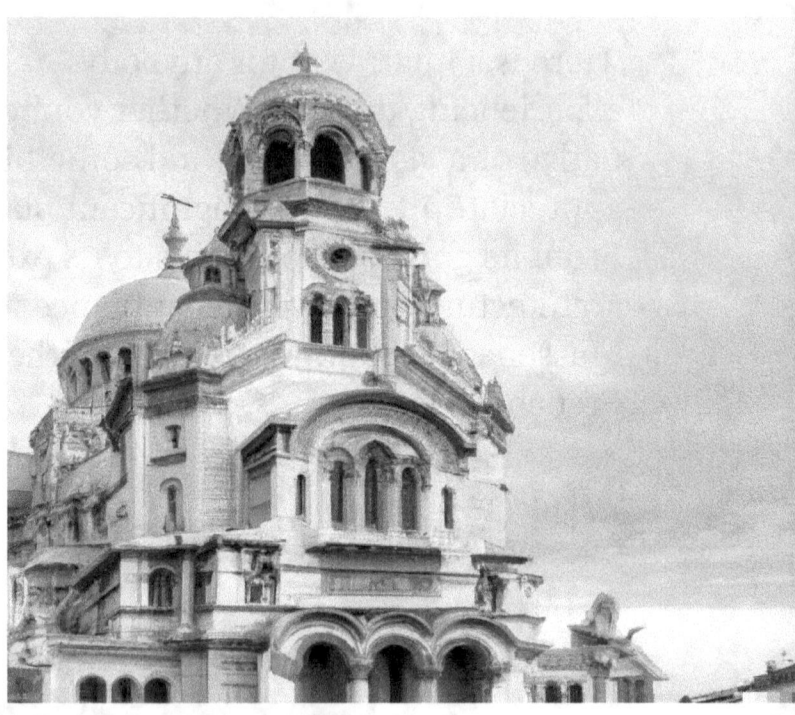

St. Nicholas Orthodox Cathedral

St. Nicholas Orthodox Cathedral is a stunning cathedral situated in Nice, France. It is a historic monument and one of the most prominent emblems of Orthodox Christianity in the nation. The cathedral was erected in the late 19th century and is recognized for its exquisite construction, gorgeous interior and rich history.

The cathedral was erected in the Neo-Byzantine style, with a central dome and two lesser domes on each side. The façade is ornamented with elaborate carvings and sculptures, while the inside is filled with vivid murals and iconography. The massive central dome rises high above the nave, flooding the area with natural light and giving the cathedral an air of grandeur.

St. Nicholas Orthodox Cathedral is also home to some of the most beautiful and historically important Orthodox Christian antiques in France. The cathedral's collection of icons, including many going back to the 16th century, is regarded as one of the greatest in the nation. The cathedral's exquisite murals, representing episodes from the life of Jesus Christ and the saints, are undoubtedly a highlight of each visit.

The history of St. Nicholas Orthodox Cathedral is strongly related to the history of Orthodox Christianity in France. The church was erected by Russian émigrés who had left their native country following the Revolution of 1917. These migrants took with them their culture, faith, and customs, and built a strong Orthodox community in Nice. Today, the cathedral remains an important site of Orthodox service and is a reminder of the rich cultural history of the Russian population in France.

Visitors to St. Nicholas Orthodox Cathedral will be captivated by the beauty and peacefulness of this ancient monument. The cathedral is accessible to tourists every day, and guided tours are offered. The cathedral's choir is especially known for its exquisite music, and visitors may frequently hear the choir singing at mass or other occasions.

St. Nicholas Orthodox Cathedral is a must-visit location for everyone interested in history, religion, or architecture. This majestic church is a monument to the endurance of the human spirit and the everlasting power of religion. Whether you are an Orthodox Christian or just interested about this interesting faith, a visit to St. Nicholas Orthodox Cathedral is bound to be a remarkable experience.

Parc Phoenix

Parc Phoenix is a botanical garden situated in Nice, France. The park was constructed in 1990 and spans an area of roughly 4.5 hectares. It is one of the biggest botanical gardens in France, featuring an incredible variety of flora from all over the globe.

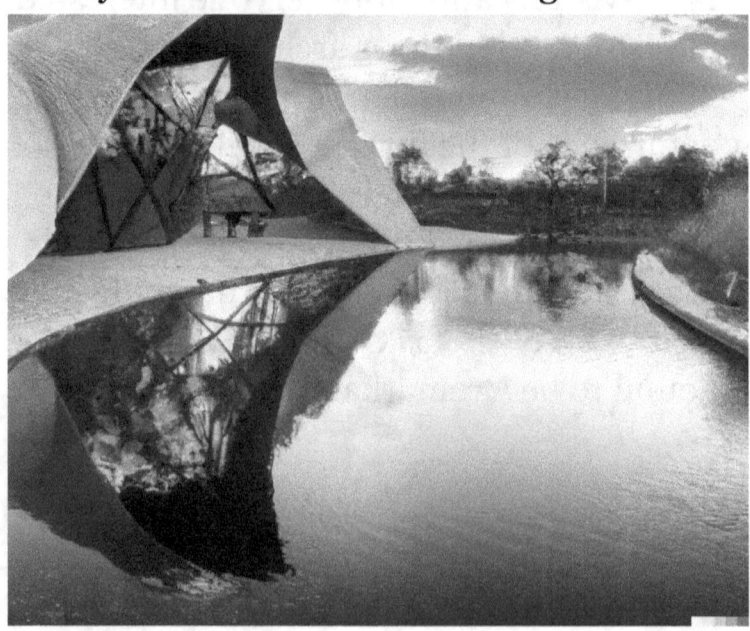

Parc Phoenix

Parc Phoenix gives a unique chance to explore and learn about a range of plants and flowers from diverse climates, including tropical, Mediterranean, and dry areas. The park has a big greenhouse that resembles a tropical forest atmosphere, as well as a vast garden with ponds, water features, and a palm grove. Visitors may also tour a cactus garden, a rose garden, and a vegetable garden.

One of the features of Parc Phoenix is its butterfly garden, where visitors can observe and interact with many kinds of butterflies from throughout the globe. In addition to the butterfly garden, there are also a variety of animal habitats, including a flamingo pond and a bird aviary. Visitors may learn about the diverse species and their habitats, as well as witness them in their natural surroundings.

Parc Phoenix also provides a range of educational events and seminars for guests of all ages. These programs span themes such as botany, gardening, and conservation, and are aimed to assist visitors learn about the significance of conserving and safeguarding the world's biodiversity.

In addition to its educational services, Parc Phoenix also functions as a location for events and exhibits. The park's huge event area and gorgeous grounds make it a perfect site for weddings, business celebrations, and other special occasions. Despite its vastness, Parc Phoenix is an easy park to traverse. Visitors may enjoy a leisurely walk around the gardens, or they can follow one of the park's numerous trails to discover the varied ecosystems and gardens. There are also various picnic sites and cafés where guests may relax and have a bite to eat.
With its magnificent gardens, diverse ecosystems, and educational activities,

visitors are guaranteed to enjoy a great and instructive time.

Musee National Marc Chagall

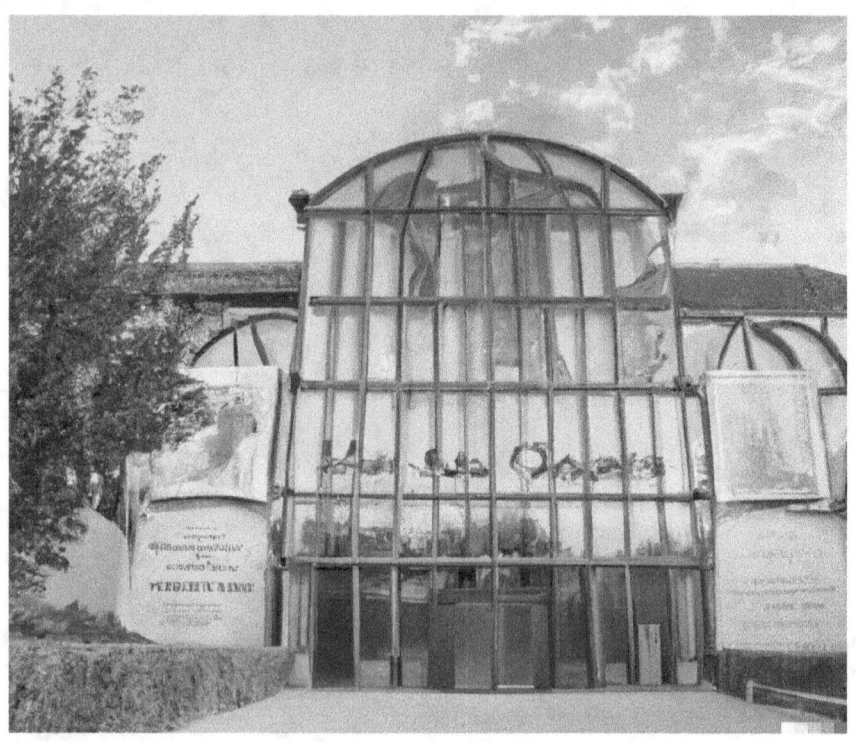

Musée National Marc Chagall exterior

The Musée National Marc Chagall is located in Nice, France and is dedicated to the works of the famous Russian-French artist, Marc Chagall. The museum, which was opened in 1973, is housed in an 18th-century villa and contains more than 3,000 works of art, including paintings, drawings, engravings, and ceramics, created by Chagall over the course of his lifetime.

Marc Chagall was born in Russia in 1887 and later moved to France, where he lived and worked for many years. He is considered one of the most important artists of the 20th century and his work is recognized for its imaginative, dream-like quality, rich colors, and fantastical subject matter. He is best known for his paintings that combine elements of cubism, futurism, and symbolism, and for his ability to create a unique and personal vision of reality that reflects his own emotions, memories, and dreams.

The Musée National Marc Chagall houses a comprehensive collection of the artist's work, including many of his most famous paintings, such as "The Green Violinist," "Over the Town," and "The Birthday." Visitors can also see a selection of Chagall's drawings, lithographs, and ceramics, as well as a number of rare and unique pieces, such as his tapestries and stained glass windows.

One of the most notable features of the museum is its architecture and setting. The museum is housed in an 18th-century villa that has been carefully restored and renovated to preserve its original character and charm. Visitors can explore the spacious galleries, gardens, and terraces, taking in the beautiful views of the Mediterranean and the city of Nice.

In addition to the permanent collection, the Musée National Marc Chagall also hosts a number of temporary exhibitions and events throughout the year, showcasing the work of other contemporary artists and designers. These exhibitions provide visitors with an opportunity to explore new perspectives on art and design and to discover new ways of looking at the world.

Visitors to the Musée National Marc Chagall can also take advantage of a range of educational programs and activities, including guided tours, workshops, and lectures. These programs are designed to help visitors of all ages understand and appreciate the art of Marc Chagall, and to deepen their understanding of the creative process.

Overall, the Musée National Marc Chagall is a must-see destination for anyone interested in the work of this iconic artist. Whether you are a lifelong admirer of Chagall's work, or simply curious to learn more about one of the most innovative artists of the 20th century, this museum is the perfect place to explore and discover the world of Marc Chagall. The Musée National Marc Chagall is a unique and fascinating institution, offering visitors the chance to delve into the world of one of the greatest artists of the 20th century.

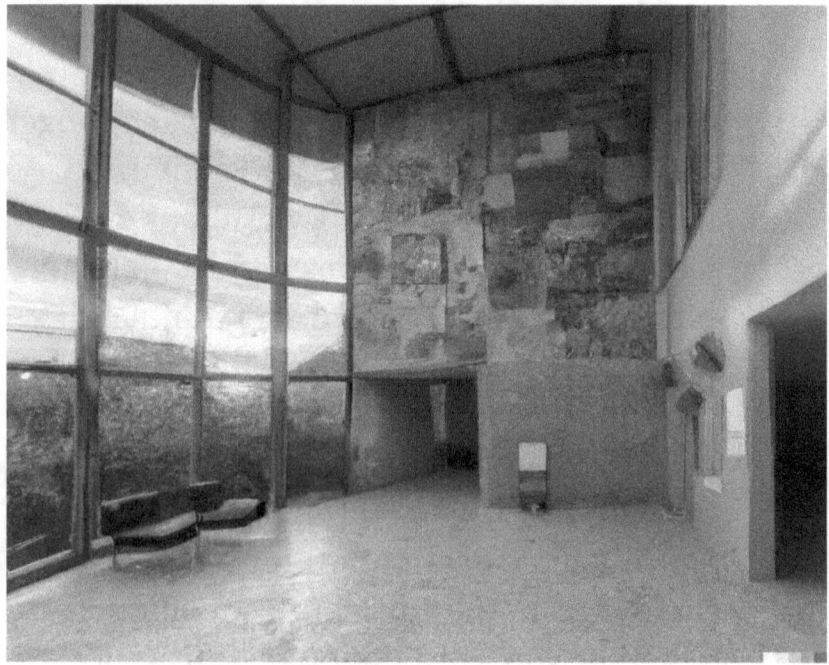

Musée National Marc Chagall interior

With its comprehensive collection of Chagall's work, its beautiful setting, and its engaging educational programs, this museum is a must-visit for anyone interested in the arts.

Nice Observatory

The Nice Observatory, situated in the city of Nice, France, is one of the world's oldest astronomical organizations. Established in 1883, the observatory has played a vital role in the study of astronomy, astrophysics, and cosmology throughout the last century.

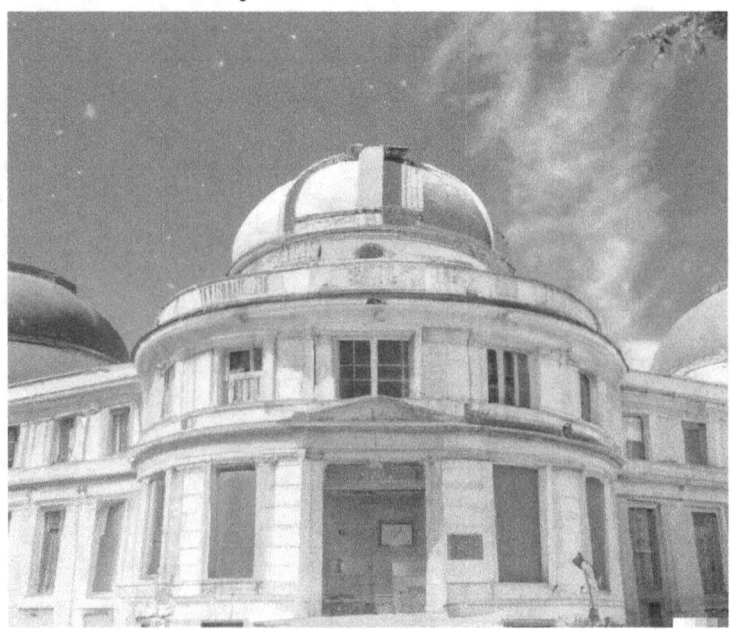

Nice Observatory

The observatory is equipped with a number of telescopes, including a 1-meter telescope, a 0.9-meter telescope, and a 0.8-meter telescope. These telescopes are used for numerous astronomical investigations, such as studying star clusters, galaxies, and supernovae. The observatory also features a variety of spectrographs, cameras, and other devices that are used to investigate the light and radiation released by celestial objects.

One of the most important successes of the Nice Observatory was the detection of the first known asteroid, Ceres, in 1801. Since then, the observatory has continued to make vital contributions to the science of astronomy. In the 20th century, the observatory was active in the research of eclipsing binary stars, which are pairs of stars that regularly eclipse each other. This

study led to a better knowledge of the structure and development of stars.
In recent years, the Nice Observatory has been at the forefront of the investigation of exoplanets, or planets that orbit stars outside of our solar system. The observatory has been involved in the identification of multiple exoplanets and has made vital contributions to our knowledge of the genesis and development of these worlds.

In addition to its scientific operations, the Nice Observatory also provides a variety of public education and outreach initiatives. The observatory has a planetarium that provides instructional events for school groups, as well as public talks and displays. The observatory also provides a summer school program for students interested in pursuing a career in astronomy.
Despite its lengthy history, the Nice Observatory remains at the forefront of

astronomy research and teaching. Its dedication to increasing our understanding of the cosmos and sharing that information with the public makes it a valued institution and a significant element of the worldwide astronomy community.

Visitors to the Nice Observatory may visit the buildings, examine the telescopes, and learn about the observatory's history and current research initiatives. The observatory is a must-visit for everyone interested in astronomy and the study of the cosmos. Whether you are a student, a scientific enthusiast, or just a curious observer, the Nice Observatory provides a unique chance to discover the marvels of the universe.

Old Nice (Vieille Ville)

Old Nice, also known as Vieille Ville, is a historic neighborhood situated in the center of Nice, France. The region is recognized for its tiny, meandering lanes, colorful houses, and lovely ambience. The history of Old Nice stretches back to the 16th century, and it has been carefully maintained to this day.

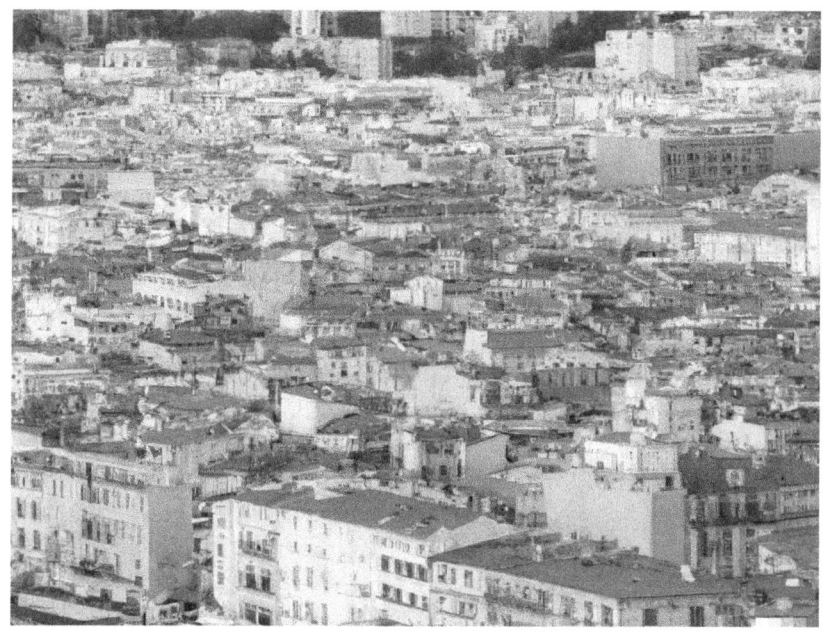
Old Nice (Vieille Ville)

The architecture of Old Nice is a variety of styles, including Baroque, Gothic, and Renaissance, and it is a real expression of the city's rich past. The buildings are embellished with elaborate embellishments, such as wrought iron balconies, stone sculptures, and paintings. The bright, pastel hues of the buildings are what give the neighborhood its trademark appeal, and they are a feast for the eyes.

One of the most recognizable structures in Old Nice is the Cathedrale Sainte-Reparate. This beautiful cathedral was erected in the 17th century and is regarded as one of the greatest examples of Baroque architecture in France. It is notable for its majestic exterior, exquisite stained glass windows, and elaborate sculptures.

The Cours Saleya is a lively market area in Old Nice and is the core of the neighborhood. It is a popular attraction for residents and visitors alike, and is recognized for its bright atmosphere and fresh products. The market takes place every day except Monday, and it is a terrific opportunity to try some of the local food.

The region is also home to a variety of museums and galleries, notably the Musee d'Art et d'Histoire de Nice, which highlights the city's rich cultural legacy. Another famous sight is the Palais Lascaris, a 17th-century palace that has been magnificently renovated and transformed into a museum.

One of the finest things about Old Nice is just getting lost in its small, twisting lanes and exploring the town on foot. There is always something new to explore, and it is a terrific opportunity to gain a sense for the city's beautiful vibe.

The region is also a popular place for shopping, and there are many boutiques and specialty stores offering anything from souvenirs to local crafts.

Old Nice is a wonderful jewel in the center of Nice, France. It is a lovely, historic quarter that gives an insight into the city's rich history and culture. Whether you are searching for architectural beauty, wonderful cuisine, or simply a quiet walk, Old Nice is a must-visit site for anybody visiting Nice.

Museum of modern and contemporary art

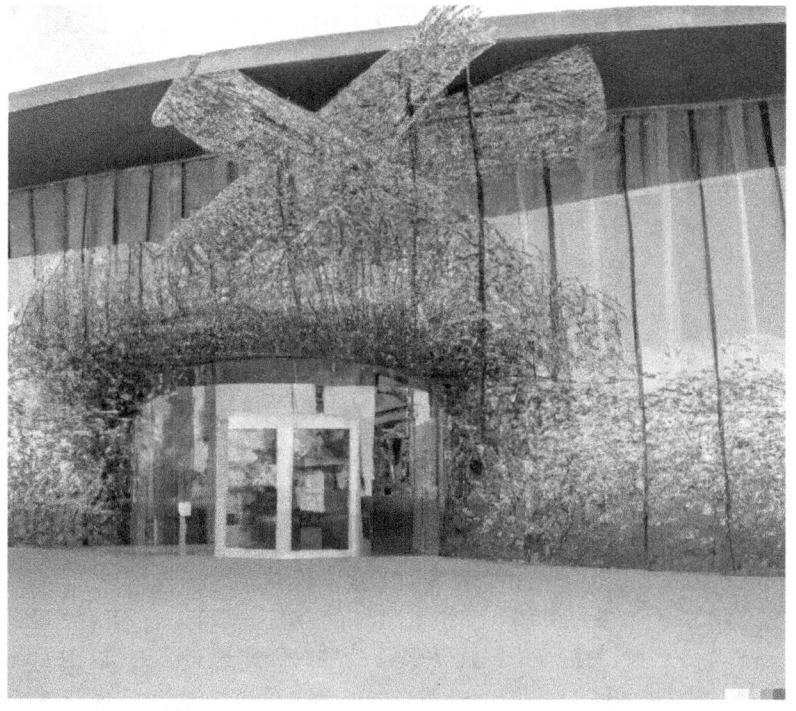

Museum of Modern and Contemporary Art in France

The Museum of Modern and Contemporary Art in France is a must-visit for art aficionados visiting the nation.

Housed in a beautiful modern structure in the center of Paris, The museum shows some of the most significant pieces of modern and contemporary art from France and throughout the globe.

The museum was formed in 1961 and has since become one of the greatest and most complete collections of modern and contemporary art in the world. It exhibits works by legendary painters such as Pablo Picasso, Henri Matisse, and Marcel Duchamp, as well as a vast collection of works by lesser-known but equally significant artists.

One of the centerpieces of the museum is its collection of Impressionist and Post-Impressionist paintings, which includes works by Claude Monet, Edgar Degas, and Pierre-Auguste Renoir. Visitors may observe the strong brushstrokes and vibrant colors that characterize these works, as well as the unique methods and styles that these painters contributed to the art world.

In addition to its amazing collection of paintings, the museum also shows a broad variety of other art genres, including sculpture, photography, and multimedia projects. Visitors may explore the many various styles and methods employed by modern artists, as well as learn about the social and cultural environment in which these works were made.

The museum's architecture and design are also worth noticing. The building itself is a modernist marvel, with its clean lines and vast glass walls affording breathtaking views of the city. Inside, the vast galleries are bright and open, giving the ideal environment for the masterpieces on show. Another notable aspect of the museum is its comprehensive educational programming, which offers workshops, lectures, and guided tours for visitors of all ages. Whether you are a seasoned art fan or merely inquisitive about the world of modern and contemporary art, there is something for everyone at this museum. The Museum of Modern and Contemporary Art in France is a must-visit location for anybody interested in the art and culture of the 20th and 21st centuries. With its world-class collection, breathtaking building, and educational programs, this museum provides a genuinely memorable experience for art enthusiasts of all ages. So, if you're in Paris, be sure to include it to your agenda.

Cimiez Monastery

Cimiez Monastery is a historic and architectural gem situated in the city of Nice, France. Founded in the 9th century, it has a rich history and a distinctive architectural style that draws thousands of visitors every year.

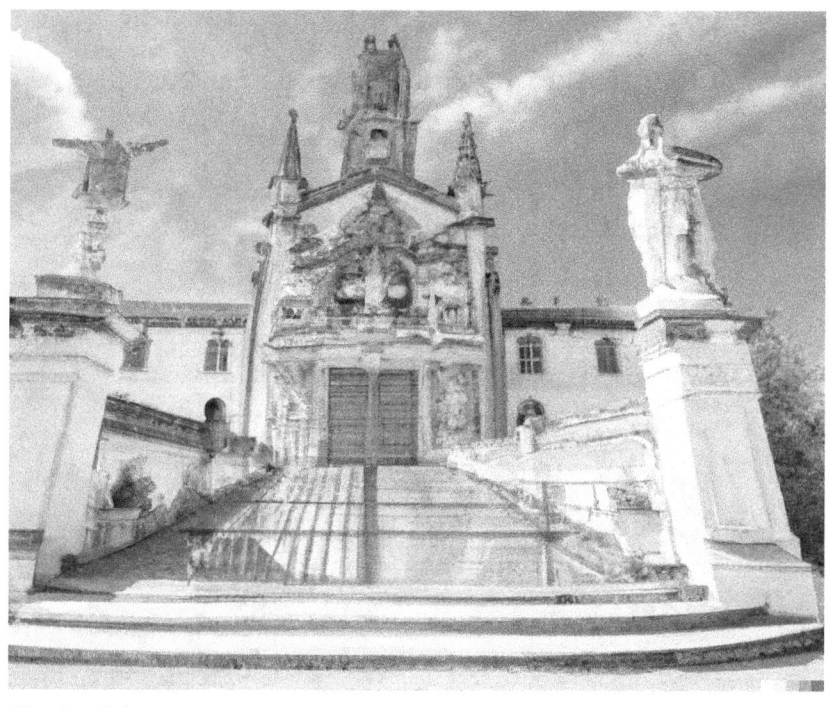

Cimiez Monastery

The Cimiez Monastery was initially founded as a Benedictine monastery in the 9th century. Over the ages, it has experienced several modifications and extensions, including the building of a church and a palace. The church, called Saint-Pons, was erected in the

Romanesque style and is now a museum presenting pieces of art and religious objects from the area. The palace, erected in the 17th century, was originally used by the bishops of Nice as a residence and is now a hotel.

One of the most prominent elements of the Cimiez Monastery is its stunning architecture. The structure shows a blend of Gothic, Renaissance and Baroque styles, making it a genuine architectural jewel. Visitors are astonished by the elaborate carvings, magnificent stained glass windows, and the spectacular murals that cover the walls and ceilings of the edifice.

Another distinctive aspect of the Cimiez Monastery is its large gardens. The gardens are separated into numerous areas, each with its own particular character and style. One of the most popular portions is the Rose Garden, which exhibits a variety of roses and other flowers arranged in exquisite arrangements. The gardens also have a variety of fountains and ponds, offering a tranquil and serene ambiance for guests to enjoy.

In addition to its architectural and landscaping elements, the Cimiez Monastery also possesses a rich cultural past. The structure has functioned as a center of scholarship and cultural exchange for centuries, drawing academics and artists from all over the globe. Today, the monastery organizes a range of cultural activities, including concerts, exhibits, and seminars.

Despite its lengthy and intriguing history, the Cimiez Monastery remains a popular tourist site. Visitors travel from all over the globe to appreciate its gorgeous architecture, enjoy its quiet gardens, and learn about its rich cultural past. Whether you're a history buff, an architectural enthusiast, or just seeking for a calm respite from the hustle and bustle of the city, the Cimiez Monastery is a must-see location for anybody visiting Nice, France.

The Cimiez Monastery is a genuine treasure of France, allowing tourists a look into the rich cultural and architectural past of the area. From its gorgeous grounds to its magnificent architecture, the monastery is likely to make a lasting impact on everyone who comes. So, if you're seeking for a really remarkable experience in Nice, be sure to add a visit to the Cimiez Monastery on your agenda.

Basilique Notre Dame de Fourvière

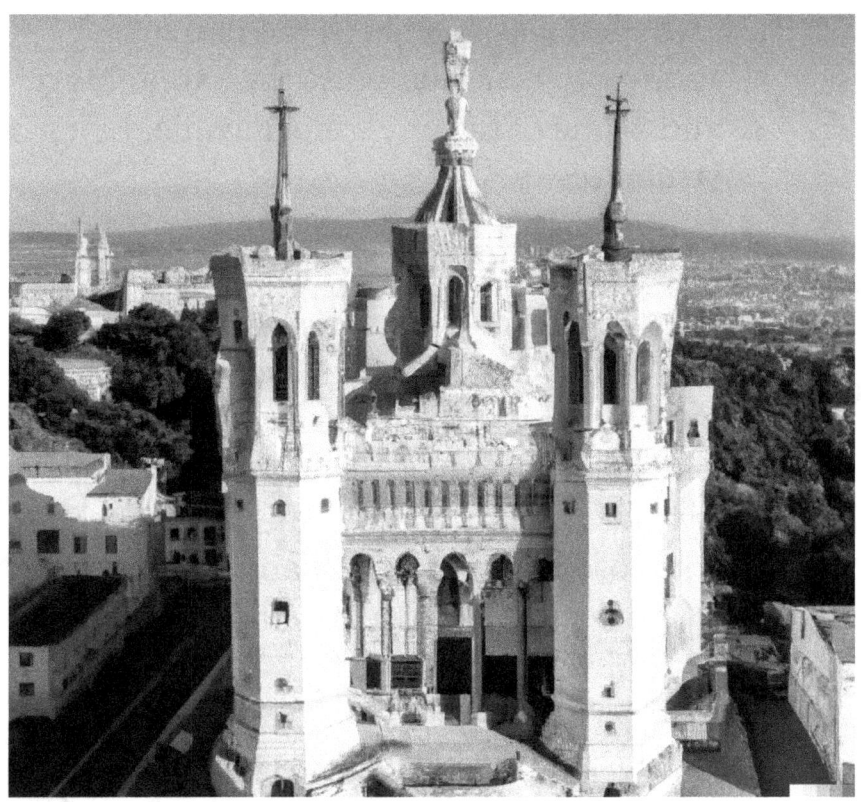

Basilique Notre-Dame de Fourvière

Basilique Notre-Dame de Fourvière is a Roman Catholic basilica situated in Lyon, France. The basilica is atop Fourvière Hill and gives panoramic views of the city. The cathedral was erected in the late 19th century to commemorate the Virgin Mary and is one of the city's most iconic structures.

Construction of the basilica started in 1872 and was finished in 1896. The architecture of the church was influenced by the architectural style of the Renaissance, with a blend of Romanesque, Gothic, and Byzantine components. The basilica is composed of white stone and contains a massive central dome, two bell towers, and a number of stained glass windows.

The inside of the basilica is equally as stunning as its appearance. The nave is adorned with columns and the walls are ornamented with murals and sculptures.

The altar is especially spectacular, built of marble and gold and containing a figure of the Virgin Mary.

One of the most prominent characteristics of Basilique Notre-Dame de Fourvière is its crypt, which holds the bones of various saints, notably Saint Joseph Marello. The crypt is a renowned pilgrimage place for Catholics and is recognized for its serene environment.

In addition to its religious importance, Basilique Notre-Dame de Fourvière is also a symbol of the city of Lyon. The basilica was created during an era of industry and modernization, and it embodies the city's faith and hope in the face of change. The basilica is also considered as a sign of optimism and a reminder of the city's Catholic past.

Visitors to the basilica may appreciate the panoramic views of the city from the summit of Fourvière Hill. The basilica is also a popular site for concerts and gatherings, with its massive central dome acting as a background for performances. Basilique Notre-Dame de Fourvière is a lovely and ancient cathedral that is a must-see for tourists visiting Lyon. Whether you are interested in architecture, religion, or history, the basilica is a unique and intriguing location that gives a look into the city's rich past and continuing character.

Place Bellecour

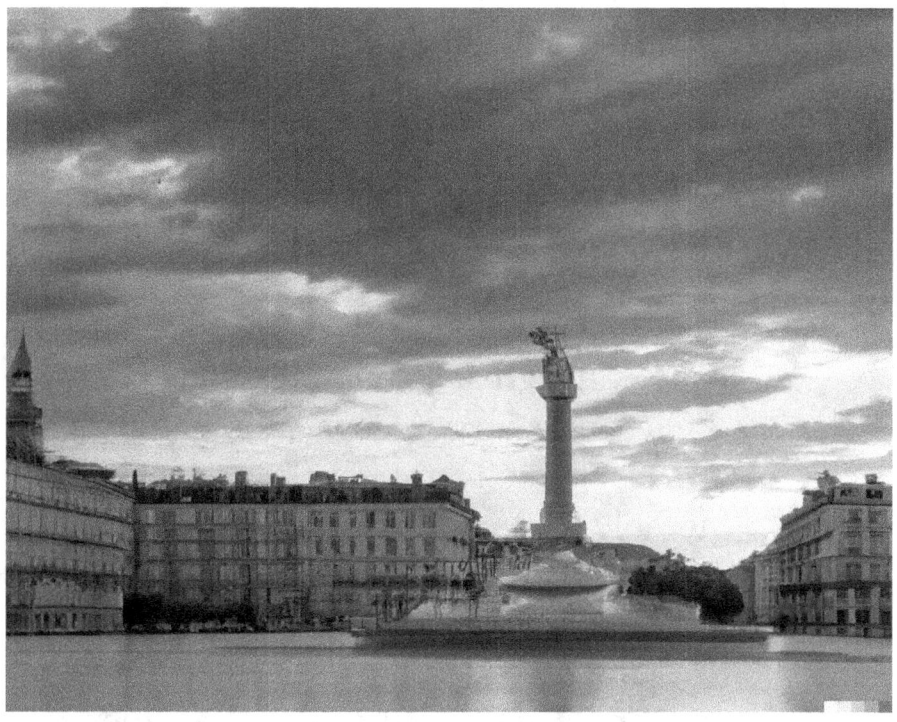

Place Bellecour

Place Bellecour is a big plaza situated in the centre of Lyon, France. It is regarded as one of the biggest public squares in Europe and is a famous tourist attraction for its gorgeous architecture, energetic atmosphere and rich history.

The square was created in the 17th century by the architect Martin Fromanger and was initially used as a marketplace. Over the years, Place Bellecour has experienced various restorations and modifications, making it the lively and energetic square it is today.

One of the great attractions of Place Bellecour is its gorgeous architecture. The area is flanked by stately structures, notably the famous Opera National de Lyon and the spectacular Hôtel de Ville. These buildings are known for their elaborate façades, magnificent sculptures and detailed decorations, making them popular sites for visitors to snap photographs.

Another famous characteristic of Place Bellecour is its bustling environment. The area is usually bursting with bustle, with street performers, merchants and artists offering entertainment for tourists. During the summer months, the area is also the venue of different outdoor concerts and festivals, making it a perfect spot to enjoy the city's cultural life.

In addition to its cultural attractions, Place Bellecour is also a popular shopping destination, with numerous stores and boutiques encircling the square. Here, tourists may discover a large selection of local and foreign goods, including apparel, jewelry, home décor, and gourmet items. Despite its hectic environment, Place Bellecour is also a calm haven in the midst of the city. The area is surrounded by beautiful flora, with large trees offering shade and a feeling of peace. Visitors may sit and rest on the benches, enjoying the sun and the views and sounds of the city. Place Bellecour is a must-visit place for anybody visiting Lyon. Its rich history, gorgeous architecture, vibrant ambiance, and serene environment make it a unique and wonderful experience. Place Bellecour provides something for everyone.

Parc de La Tête d'Or

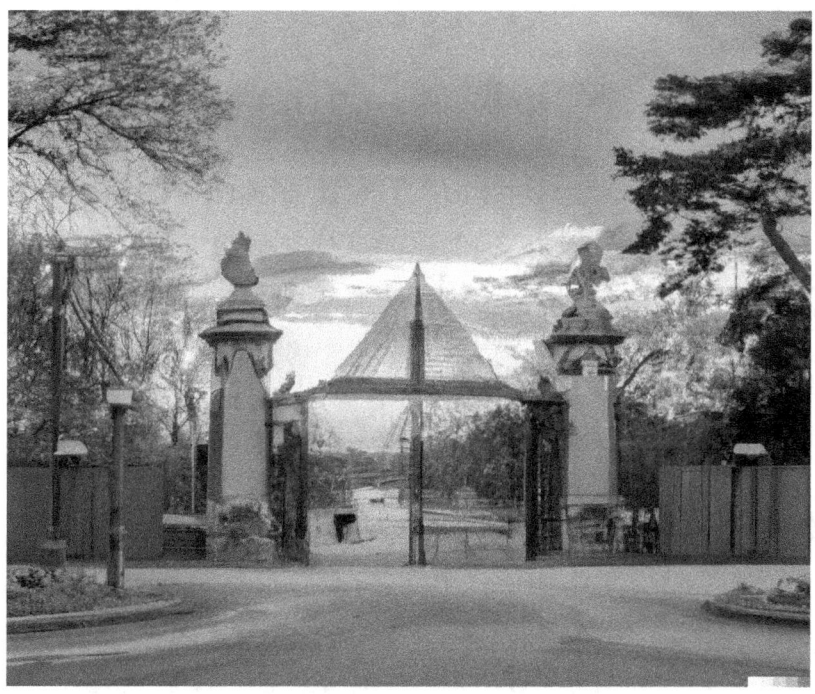

Parc de La Tête d'Or

Parc de La Tête d'Or is a public park situated in the centre of Lyon, France. It encompasses an area of approximately 117 hectares and is one of the biggest city parks in Europe. The park was founded in

1857 and has been a popular attraction for residents and tourists alike for over 150 years.

One of the most prominent aspects of Parc de La Tête d'Or is its enormous lake, which occupies an area of about 20 hectares. The lake is surrounded by walking and cycling routes, and tourists may hire boats or join a guided tour by boat. The lake is also home to a variety of species, including ducks, geese, and swans.

The park is particularly notable for its botanical garden, which was built in 1857 and features a vast range of plants, trees, and flowers from across the globe. There is a big greenhouse that contains exotic plants, as well as various outdoor gardens that exhibit the beauty of French gardening. The botanical garden is a renowned location for nature enthusiasts and people interested in botany.

In addition to its natural beauty, Parc de La Tête d'Or also provides a selection of leisure activities. There are various sports fields and courts, including tennis and basketball, as well as a playground for children. Visitors may also hire bicycles or rollerblades to explore the park's various routes and trails.

One of the most remarkable characteristics of Parc de La Tête d'Or is its mini-zoo, which is home to a variety of animals, including monkeys, deer, and camels. The mini-zoo is a popular location for families with children and individuals interested in nature.

The park is also a popular site for events and gatherings, including concerts, festivals, and athletic activities. There is a big open-air theater that presents a variety of acts throughout the year, as well as various picnic sites where guests may relax and enjoy a meal.

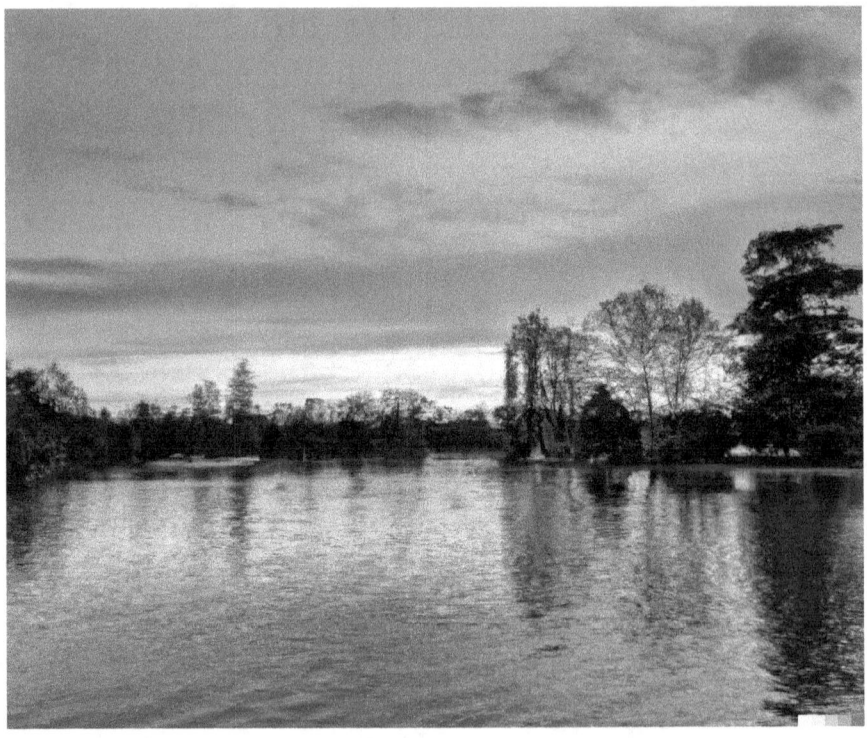

Parc de La Tête d'Or is a lovely public park that provides something for everyone. Whether you are interested in nature, sports, culture, or just seeking a place to unwind, this park offers it all. Its beauty, history, and choice of activities make it a must-visit location for anybody visiting Lyon.

Miniature museum and theater

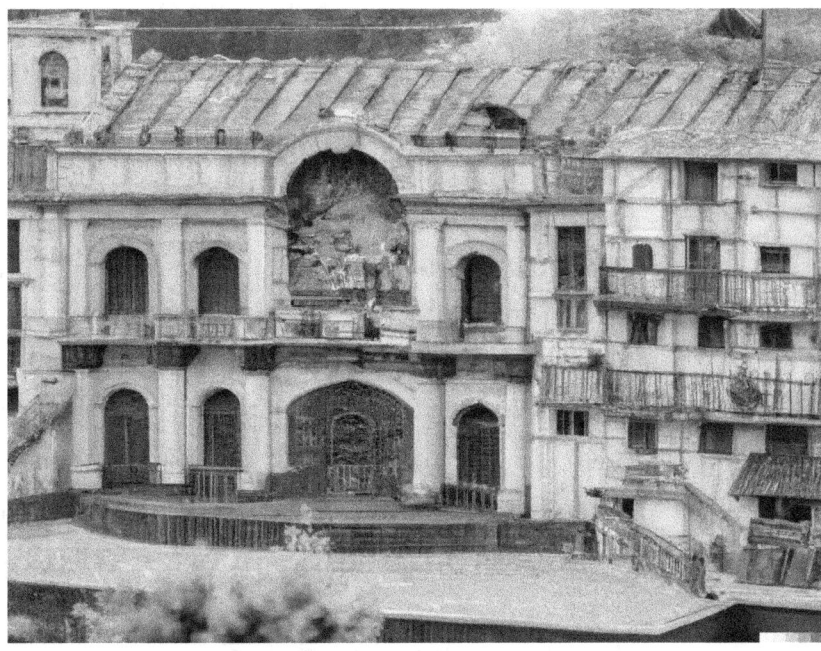

The Miniature museum and theatre

The Miniature Museum and Theater in France is a unique and intriguing site for tourists of all ages. Located in the center of Paris, this museum provides an immersive experience that highlights the art and skill of tiny models and dioramas.

The museum displays a broad variety of exhibits, from elaborate doll houses and model trains to accurate miniature theaters and cinemas. Visitors may marvel at the elaborate detailing and delicate workmanship of each item, which span from antique re-creations to modern designs.

One of the features of the museum is the Miniature Theater, a fully working theater that puts on a variety of events throughout the year. These productions are presented by professional performers who bring to life a variety of classic and current plays and musicals, all set inside a small setting.

With its detailed sets, complex lighting, and attention to detail, the Miniature Theater is a genuinely wonderful experience.

Visitors may also explore the museum's enormous collection of miniature movie scenes, which highlight the art of film-making on a tiny size. These models, which vary from basic cardboard sets to elaborate metal and plastic sculptures, provide a view into the world of movie-making and provide a fascinating contrast to the larger-scale films that we are all acquainted with.

Another attraction of the museum is its collection of miniature museums, which are perfect reproductions of some of the world's most renowned museums and galleries. These replicas, which include notable institutions like the Louvre and the British Museum, enable visitors to experience the art and architecture of these great buildings in a whole new manner.

In addition to its exhibitions, the Miniature Museum and Theater also provides a selection of seminars and courses for guests of all ages. Whether you're an ambitious model builder, a film enthusiast, or just seeking for a fun and instructive experience, the museum offers something for everyone.

So if you're seeking for a unique and intriguing experience in Paris, make sure to visit the Miniature Museum and Theater. Whether you're a history buff, an art enthusiast, or just a fan of all things little, this museum is guaranteed to capture and thrill you. So why wait? Plan your visit now and experience the wonder of this one-of-a-kind museum!

Cathedral Saint Jean Baptiste

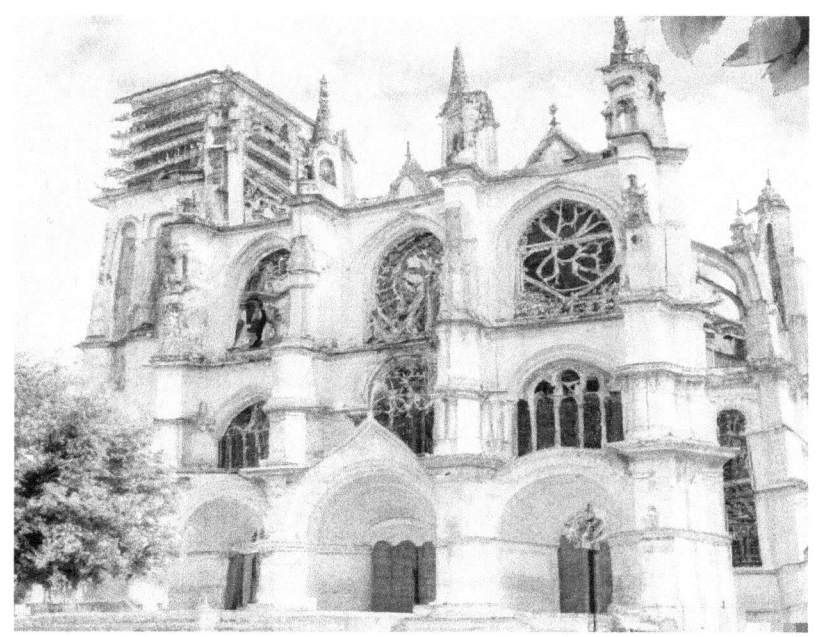

Cathedral Saint Jean Baptiste

The Pyramid of Saint Jean Baptiste is a significant monument found in the city of Clermont-Ferrand in Auvergne, France. It was created in the 19th century as a monument to Saint John the Baptist, the patron saint of Clermont-Ferrand. The pyramid is a prominent tourist site and draws tourists from all over the globe.

The Pyramid of Saint Jean Baptiste was erected between 1855 and 1863 and rises at a height of 33 meters. It was created by the French architect, Jacques-Ignace Hittorff, and is regarded as a masterpiece of French architecture. The pyramid is composed of stone and has elaborate carvings, sculptures, and stained glass windows. The pyramid is fashioned like a cross, representing the crucifixion of Saint John the Baptist, and is regarded one of the most magnificent religious structures in France.

The inside of the pyramid is equally as spectacular as the façade. Visitors are met by a lovely nave that is lit by stained glass windows. The nave is encircled by chapels and shrines that pay honor to Saint John the Baptist and other saints. The walls of the pyramid are covered with sculptures and paintings that portray incidents from the life of Saint John the Baptist.

The Pyramid of Saint Jean Baptiste is also an important religious site. Every year, hundreds of people from all over France assemble to the pyramid to commemorate the feast of Saint John the Baptist. The feast is a happy and holy celebration that involves a parade, mass, and other festivities.

In addition to its religious importance, the Pyramid of Saint Jean Baptiste is also a significant historical landmark. It is a testimony to the rich cultural legacy of the Auvergne area and the city of Clermont-Ferrand. The pyramid has been well-preserved throughout the years and is a wonderful example of French architecture and religious art.

Visitors to the Pyramid of Saint Jean Baptiste may also explore the surrounding region, which is home to many other noteworthy sights. The city of Clermont-Ferrand is noted for its historical and cultural monuments, including the Notre-Dame-du-Port Basilica, the Saint-Pierre-des-Minimes chapel, and the Clermont-Ferrand Cathedral.

The Pyramid of Saint Jean Baptiste is a must-visit location for everyone going to the Auvergne area of France. Its elaborate architecture, lovely interior, and rich theological and cultural history make it a really exceptional location. Whether you are a devoted believer, a history buff, or simply someone who enjoys beauty and grandeur, the Pyramid of Saint Jean

Baptiste is likely to create a lasting impression.

Zoo De Lyon

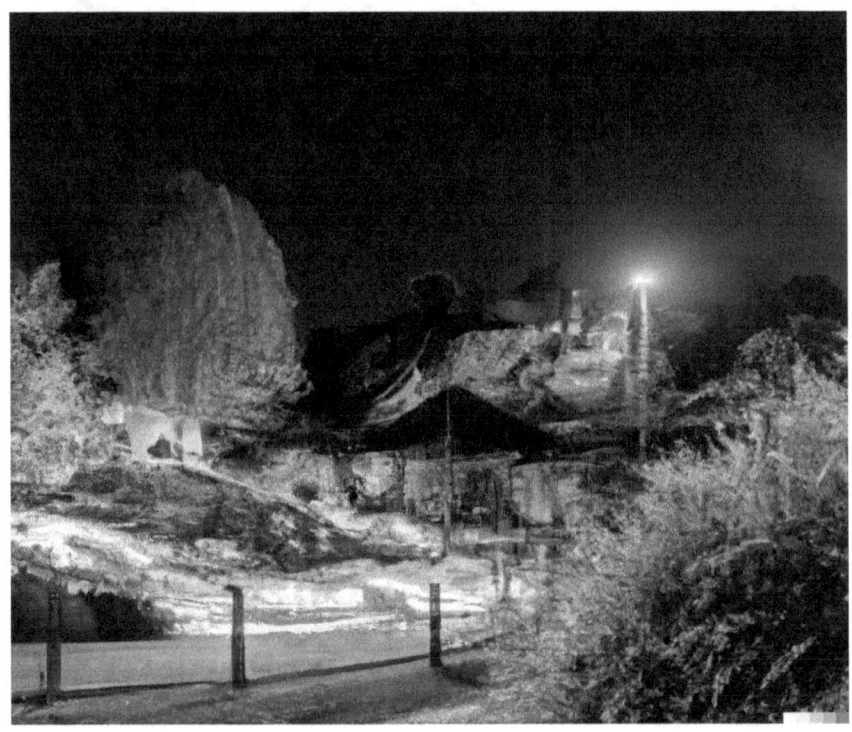

Zoo De Lyon

Zoo de Lyon, located in the heart of Lyon, France, is a unique and fascinating destination for visitors of all ages. Established in 1934, it is one of the oldest zoos in France and is home to over 800 animals from all over the world, including a diverse array of mammals, birds, reptiles, and insects.

One of the main attractions of Zoo de Lyon is its large and diverse collection of primates, including gorillas, chimpanzees, and orangutans. Visitors can observe these intelligent and social animals in their natural habitats, which are designed to mimic the conditions of the rainforest. These habitats allow visitors to see the primates up close and to understand more about their behavior and social dynamics.

Another highlight of Zoo de Lyon is its bird park, which is home to a wide variety of species from around the world, including colorful parrots, graceful flamingos, and majestic birds of prey. Visitors can observe the birds in their aviaries or, during special shows, see them in flight. The zoo also has a large collection of reptiles, including snakes, lizards, and turtles, as well as a variety of insects and arachnids.

In addition to its animal collections, Zoo de Lyon offers a range of educational and interactive experiences for visitors. These include guided tours, animal encounters, and hands-on workshops, which allow visitors to learn about the different species and the importance of conservation. The zoo also offers a variety of seasonal events, such as Halloween celebrations and Christmas lights displays, which add to the fun and excitement of a visit.

One of the most unique and innovative features of Zoo de Lyon is its "Biozoo" exhibit, which is designed to highlight the biodiversity of the planet and the importance of conservation. The exhibit features a range of habitats, including a tropical rainforest, a desert, and a savanna, and allows visitors to observe and learn about the different species and ecosystems found in these regions.

Zoo de Lyon is also committed to conservation and sustainability, and is actively involved in a number of breeding and conservation programs for endangered species. The zoo also works with local and international organizations to support conservation efforts and raise awareness about the importance of protecting the world's biodiversity.

Zoo de Lyon is a must-visit destination for anyone interested in wildlife and conservation. With its diverse collection of animals, interactive exhibits, and commitment to conservation, it offers a unique and unforgettable experience for visitors of all ages. Whether you're a seasoned zoo-goer or a first-time visitor,

Zoo de Lyon is sure to be a highlight of your time in Lyon.

Money-saving Tips For You

1. Plan ahead: Before you go, investigate the greatest rates on flights, hotels, and transportation. Look for offers and discounts on travel websites and sign up for email notifications from airlines and hotels.

2. Use public transit: France has a large public transportation system, including trains, buses, and metro systems. This is a cost-effective method to move about and may save you money on rental vehicles or taxis.

3. Book lodgings in advance: Booking your hotel or vacation rental in advance might save you money. Look

for offers and discounts on travel websites or try staying in a hostel or Airbnb.

4. Pack a picnic: France is famed for its great cuisine, but dining out may be pricey. Consider taking a picnic lunch and snacks to save money on meals.

5. Take advantage of free activities: France offers numerous free activities such as parks, museums, and historic places. Do your study and arrange your schedule to take advantage of these free activities.

6. Use discount cards: If you want to visit numerous museums or other sites, consider buying a Paris Museum Pass or City Pass. These cards provide discounts and might save you money in the long term.

7. Be cautious of currency conversion rates: France utilizes the Euro, therefore be mindful of currency exchange rates while making purchases. Look for ATMs that give the best conversion rates and consider using a credit card that doesn't charge international transaction fees.

8. Shop at local markets: France is famed for its markets, where you can get local fruit, cheese, bread, and other things for a fraction of the cost of supermarkets.

9. Avoid high tourist season: Consider vacationing during the shoulder season, when rates are cheaper and crowds are lighter.

10. Be open to alternate options: Instead of staying in high-end hotels, try staying in smaller, family-run guesthouses or bed & breakfasts, which are typically more economical.

What to expect when you are in France.

Monday through Friday in France, many individuals normally work or attend school. Most shops and companies are open during normal business hours, however some may have shortened hours on Saturdays. Public transit is normally accessible throughout the week, although on a limited schedule on weekends.

On Saturdays, many shops and companies are open, although again may have fewer hours than during the week. It's an excellent day to do some shopping.

On Sundays, most shops and companies are closed. Some stores and pharmacies may be open, but many people utilize this day to spend time with family and friends, or to attend church. Public transit is normally accessible on a restricted timetable.

It's also worth mentioning that many establishments in France shut for a few hours in the middle of the day for lunch.

In conclusion, Volume 1 of the France travel guide has offered a complete overview of the various features and attractions of this wonderful nation. From the busy streets of Paris to the picturesque towns of the countryside, France is a destination like no other, providing something for everyone. Whether you're interested in art, history, gastronomy, or simply soaking up the local culture, this book has offered essential information and recommendations to help you organize your trip.

As we approach the conclusion of Volume 1, it's evident that there is still much more to know about France. In preparation of Volume 2, we look forward to exploring even more of this great nation and sharing our discoveries with you. From the magnificent beaches of the French Riviera to the lovely vineyards of the Loire Valley to different cuisine and drinks, there is so much more to explore and enjoy. Stay tuned for Volume 2, as we continue to unearth the many treasures of France.

www.ingramcontent.com/pod-product-compliance
Lightning Source LLC
Chambersburg PA
CBHW052345220526
45465CB00003BA/956